Anointed to Reign

David's Pathway to Rulership

Anointed to Reign

David's Pathway to Rulership

Ronald E. Cottle, Ph.D, Ed.D

Destiny Image® Publishers, Inc.
P.O. Box 310
Shippensburg, PA 17257-0310

"Speaking to the Purposes of God for This Generation and for the Generations to Come"

ISBN 1-56043-176-8

For Worldwide Distribution
Printed in the U.S.A.

Destiny Image books are available through these fine distributors outside the United States:

Christian Growth, Inc.
Jalan Kilang-Timor, Singapore 0315

Omega Distributors
Ponsonby, Auckland, New Zealand

Rhema Ministries Trading
Randburg, Rep. of South Africa

Salvation Book Centre
Petaling, Jaya, Malaysia

Vine Christian Centre
Mid Glamorgan, Wales, United Kingdom

WA Buchanan Company
Geebung, Queensland, Australia

Word Alive
Niverville, Manitoba, Canada

This book and all other Destiny Image
and Treasure House books
are available at Christian bookstores everywhere.

Call for a bookstore nearest you.
1-800-722-6774
Or reach us on the Internet: **http://www.reapernet.com**

Contents

Introduction

Without a word, the old priest-judge Samuel brought forth his vial and opened it as he had done once before. Then he poured the oil on the head of the ruddy shepherd boy before the eyes of his astounded family. This solemn ceremony of anointing marked the beginning of young David's preparation to be king of Israel after Saul.

Years before, the old prophet had anointed another young man, a man who stood head and shoulders above his peers, a man with even more outward appearances of promise and potential than David. However, unlike David, Saul's day of anointing did not mark the beginning of a course of training for his calling. He stepped instead directly from the shadows of obscurity into a seat of power and reigned without being trained—with disastrous results. Without a doubt, Samuel must have been thinking about Saul the day he anointed David in obedience to the word of the Lord:

And the Lord said unto Samuel, How long wilt thou mourn for Saul, seeing I have rejected him from reigning over Israel? fill thine horn with oil, and go, I will send thee to Jesse the Bethlehemite: for I have provided Me a king among his sons (1 Samuel 16:1).

"I have *rejected* him from *reigning* over Israel." God did not reject Saul as a king; He rejected the quality of his reign. Saul was still the king of Israel and the anointed of God, but he was out of fellowship with God. God may not reject you from being His son, but He will certainly reject your lifestyle if it is sinful. Anyone who willfully pursues a lifestyle of sin or disobedience will strain and may ultimately break *fellowship* without breaking *relationship* with God.

Saul's willful sin broke fellowship with both God and Samuel. He literally broke Samuel's heart, just as the prophet's sons had done. Samuel had grown up in the house of Eli the priest after being born as a "child of prayer" who was "devoted" to the Lord by his grateful mother. Eli's sons, on the other hand, were tempestuous, crude, and greedy—or in a word, demonic. You would never think Samuel's would grow up to be rogues just like Eli's sons, but sadly enough, they did. In the end, they ripped their father's heart to shreds.

I'm sure that when Saul came into Samuel's life this disappointed father thought, *I am finally going to have a son who will be obedient to God, a son I can be proud of. Here is someone in whom I can invest myself.* I think Samuel hoped Saul would carry on his prophetic legacy in his own generation. In other words, Saul was to be Samuel's *spiritual* son through God's genetics and spiritual lineage.

Samuel had renewed hope that Saul would be his son, but to his dismay, Saul miserably failed him like everybody else had done. Samuel was mourning for Saul because he loved him. He had anointed Saul king at the insistence of the people of Israel, and when Saul failed so miserably, Samuel went back home and built a school of the prophets. He kept busy teaching, studying, working, and performing his ministry, but God had a greater plan and purpose for His people and His prophet. He told His sad-faced servant, "Stop your mourning. Fill your horn with oil...."

In the end, by the time of Samuel's death, he wound up with only one son—David. Though little was written in the Bible about the relationship between Samuel and David, what is written says a lot. A casual or light reading may easily bypass the close, trusting relationship Samuel had with David, but in fact, they enjoyed a very close relationship.

"Fill thine horn with *oil* and go." The Hebrew word for "oil" in this passage is *shemen*. It means "God's character and nature in the capability of imparting it." In other words, God's divine anointing oil represented His creative ability inside a man's life. When God ordained the prophet to anoint a man to be the king of Israel, He was saying, "I am giving him a measure of My nature and character, My spiritual genetics, to become and to accomplish that to which I've called him." Just as a human father passes on his characteristics, bloodline, and nature to his children through natural genetics, God passes on His characteristics through His spiritual genetics.

"I will send thee to Jesse the Bethlehemite: for I have *provided* Me a king among his sons." The Hebrew word for "provided" is *ra'ah*, and it means "to see" or "to see the depths." It is derived from the word *ra' eh* (seeing or experiencing) and *ro' eh* (seer). When God said, "I have *provided* [*ra' ah*] Me a king," He said three primary things:

1. "I have already *produced* Myself a king." God already knew when, how, and why Saul would fail. God did not cause or predetermine Saul's downfall, nor did He "push him away" because David came along. He *foreknew* that Saul, the man chosen by the people would fail. Saul was a "man after man's own heart." God's remedy for man's folly was to raise up a man after His own heart. He produced David before the foundations of the world as we will see further on.

2. "I have already *prepared* and chosen Myself a king." Only seven of Jesse's eight sons were presented to Samuel. Eliab, the eldest son, was tall, fair, and probably the most attractive. Samuel thought, *Surely this must be the one*, but the Lord told Samuel, "...Look not on his countenance, or on the height of his stature; because I have refused him: for the Lord seeth not as man seeth; for man looketh on the outward appearance, but the Lord looketh on the heart" (1 Sam. 16:7). This divine approach still confounds the world today.

   One by one, the old prophet examined and dismissed each of Jesse's seven sons. Samuel knew he had not seen the chosen king. Finally he asked Jesse if there were any more sons, and the one who remained, the youngest, the keeper of the sheep, was brought in from the fields to stand before Samuel. Immediately the prophet knew this was the man God had sent him to anoint. God had already made him a king, he was living in the house of Jesse, and everything about him was known to God.

3. "I am ready now to *present* Myself a king." When God has a word of knowledge or wisdom, or a prophetic word for a prophet, God first produces and prepares it before bringing it to a "presentation point." At that "ready" point, He brings it to the "womb" of the prophet's mouth, and thus it is presented to God.

Then Samuel took the horn of oil, and anointed him in the midst of his brethren: and the spirit of the Lord came upon David from that day forward... (1 Samuel 16:13).

"Then Samuel took the horn of oil, and *anointed* him in the midst of his brethren." The Hebrew word for "anointed" is *mashach*. I've heard people say this word means, very simply, "to rub." Now, there is another word that means "to rub on oil," and it generally describes anointing for medicinal purposes. The term as it is used in this passage very often means "to pour," to pour on. Those who were *mashach* were set apart for God's service and chosen by Him. It meant they were authorized and sent by Him, and His Spirit was with them. It is from *mashach* that we get the term *Messiah*, meaning "the conclusive and ultimate One whom God authorized and sent, and with whom His Spirit dwelt."

"And the spirit of the Lord came upon David from that day forward." The anointing that came *from* Samuel *onto* David was the *shemen Yahweh*. The creative oil of the nature and character of God Himself came onto David when Samuel anointed (*mashach*) David. He poured the oil on his head and laid his hands on him. When he did, the Spirit of the Lord came upon David. From that day forward, the Spirit of God filled his life.

God gave us David's life as a master model for aspiring and active leaders today. Indeed, David's humble path from the fields of Judea to the throne of Israel makes him the paragon of leadership. His calling, training, and rule reveal invaluable principles of leadership for us as we train to reign in fulfillment of our calling.

Ron Cottle
Columbus, Georgia
1996

Part I

Bethlehem: The House of Bread

The Place of Calling, Anointing, and Beginning

Chapter 1

David Finds a King to Serve

If the Church and the followers of Jesus are anointed to rule and reign in this life, then why do we have to "go back to school" through trials and afflictions? Why can't we just start "reigning" right now? The truth is that we all have a problem with *kaka*. (You read it correctly—I said, "*kaka*.")

Jesus has planted His seed of God-likeness in your spirit, but there are two other parts of your makeup. You *are* a soul, you *have* a spirit, and you *live* in a body. When Jesus entered your life He planted the seed of your divine design, and He restored your God-likeness inside of your spirit man, where it has been growing ever since.

That seed of destiny in your inner man may be having a hard time because your soul is full of something the original Greek language called *kakos*! Do you know what *kakos* is? If you speak Spanish, you may be surprised to learn the Greek term, *kakos* means the same thing that *kaka* does in Spanish—except it refers to soulish filthiness instead of the physical version. Frankly, you're loaded with it—you're full of it, and so am I! We're all full of *kakos*. As the divine destiny and divine design of God continue to grow within us, they erase and transform all of the ugly things hidden inside us. The Bible says in James 1, "Wherefore lay apart all filthiness and superfluity of naughtiness [*kakia*], and receive with meekness the engrafted word, which is able to save your souls" (Jas. 1:21).

So as the divine design grows, we become more and more like Him, the perfect pattern of our destiny. The Bible says, "What? know ye not that your body is the temple of the Holy Ghost which is in you, which ye have of God, and ye are not your own?" (1 Cor. 6:19) The Holy Spirit comes upon us from the inside, from our spirit man. The Greek word *baptizo* means "to whelm or to overwhelm." The Holy Spirit comes like "rivers of living water" to flood and inundate our being, allowing us to live and move and have our being in Him (see Jn. 7:38; Acts 17:28).

We are all the rightful heirs and occupants of some throne of authority in the divine Kingdom. The only reason we're not there is that we have some training to complete before we can get there. Life is a series of classrooms, clearinghouses, and training centers to help us become who we are in God.

Our "classroom" experiences may seem to be easy, but the clearinghouse experiences can be tough; because that is where we are required to lose a lot of *kakos*. It is the fear and pain involved with leaving our *kakos* behind that keeps us from achieving, or fulfilling, our destiny, isn't it?

David's life demonstrates a crucial fact of life in God's Kingdom: *We must train in the Church before we can reign in*

Zion. We must all go through three classrooms, clearing-houses, and supply centers and learn the three major lessons to be learned in each of these arenas of training. The classrooms of David that we must face today are found at Bethlehem, Adullam, and Hebron. How well are you progressing? Where are you in your journey? What are you learning right now?

① The first classroom takes place in Bethlehem. This Hebrew name is composed of two root words: *beth* means "house," and *lehem* means "bread." Bethlehem is "the house of bread." It is your home church, the place where you eat the bread of God's Word. This is where you get the "basics" inside you, so you can grow into who and what you are called to be.

I was born and reared in Columbus, Georgia. I hardly ever left the four-to-five block area around my house until I was six or seven years old. When I travel through that small area now, I'm always amazed at the way my memory just explodes. Ninety percent of my personality and inner being was formed in the first seven years of my life. It is amazing to think about how my formation literally took place within a five-square block area—my "Bethlehem" if you will. My home church was right there, and what was formed in me there is still in me, and will always be there.

Bethlehem is the place of calling. It is the place of anointing and beginning. Bethlehem represents the *nepios* or *neophyte* stage—the early stage of David's training process. The same is true for you and me today.

Now, I want to say something that I'll say again when we come to Adullam, and again when we come to Hebron.

Learn your lessons well at Bethlehem. You must learn the three major lessons of Bethlehem if you ever want to reign in Zion.

At Bethlehem these lessons will be relatively easy to learn, but if you don't learn them, or if you postpone them until later on, they will become a source of embarrassment and devastation in your life! Most people in the ministry who "fall" into sin failed to learn some "Bethlehem lesson" at Bethlehem and were forced to learn it later in their lives when the "stakes" (and pain levels) were higher.

The recent history of the Church has provided far too many examples demonstrating the consequences of allowing basic lessons to go unlearned. Those unlearned lessons will follow you from one classroom to the next. If you are ever going to be anything in the Kingdom, you will have to learn the basic lessons.

The first major lesson of Bethlehem is the lesson of *spiritual authority.* David's very first act after he caught a glimpse of his destiny and felt the touch of God's anointing was to *find a king to serve.* He came under spiritual authority. "And David came to Saul, and stood before him: and he loved him greatly; and he became [Saul's] armourbearer" (1 Sam. 16:21).

I try to read major portions of Watchman Nee's great book, *Spiritual Authority*, every year. It stays within arm's length of my desk in my study. He wrote, "There is no one who is fit to be God's delegated authority in the kingdom, unless he himself first knows how to be under authority."

David knew this. That is why he obediently came under the authority of the reigning king. Watchman Nee also said, "If any one of [God's] children is independent and self-reliant, not subject to God's delegated authority, then that one can never accomplish the work of God on earth."

God doesn't have any "lone rangers." He has created a Body as His habitation, and we were created and ordained to function as members joined together within His Body, the Church. Every high throne of authority or ministry in the Kingdom begins as a humble seat of servanthood in the Church. Authority in the Kingdom only comes out of ministry. Ministry is really servanthood, isn't it? The greater the servant, the greater the authority. The greater the authority, the greater the servant.

⊛ You can never be in the Kingdom what you do not become in the Church. The way you behave in the local "Bethlehem" church writes the blueprint of what you will be in the Kingdom. I've heard many people say, "If I were just an evangelist, or maybe a pastor or an apostle…if I were a prophet, then I'd be one of the greatest." Yet they don't even come to prayer meetings on Wednesday nights, and they don't even pay their tithes!

They don't even try to influence anybody to come to the Lord Jesus through the local church. If they had the position they wanted right now in their local church, they would be the same sorry thing they are now—that is why God won't give them that position. You have to prove yourself here (at home in Bethlehem) before God will put you there (on the throne in Zion). ⊛

David somehow sensed the importance of this principle. According to First Samuel 16:21, "David came to

Saul...." We don't have "reigning kings" in the political sense in America today, but we do have God-ordained apostolic authority or delegated authority in our local churches. God wants to impart training and wisdom from His seasoned men and women to His young trainees for Kingdom leadership.

The Bible says, "David stood before Saul." That may not sound terribly important, but the Hebrew word translated as "to stand" is *yatsav*. It means "to station oneself before" or to stand or offer oneself to another for service. David came to Saul and said, "What can I do to serve you? What can I do to become a part of the kingdom?"

Psalm 134:1 says, "Behold, bless ye the Lord, all ye servants of the Lord, which by night stand in the house of the Lord." The writer isn't talking about a bunch of people standing around in a temple all night—he is talking about those who present themselves to God for service. The priests under the old covenant sometimes swept the floors, and cleaned up the splattered blood of the sacrifices. At times they had to skin the animals, remove the refuse from the area, and keep the candles lit and the wicks trimmed. All of these services qualify as "standing" before the Lord.

David presented himself to Saul, and he did whatever his hand found to do. In Joshua 1:1, the Bible describes Joshua as Moses' "minister" (*sharath* in the Hebrew). *Sharath* means "valet, personal servant." It refers to someone who comes to another and says, "What can I do to participate in what God is doing in your life and ministry?"

In First Kings 19:19, the Bible says that Elijah found Elisha plowing a field with twelve yoke of oxen. This shows us that Elisha's papa must have been rich. The oxen must have belonged to Elisha's papa because a servant couldn't have done what Elisha did. This man was plowing with the twelfth yoke of oxen when Elijah suddenly went to him, threw his mantle over him, and just kept on walking!

The old prophet didn't say a word, but Elisha knew what had happened. He had caught a glimpse of his destiny and felt a touch of that anointing. He immediately ran after Elijah and said, "Elijah, wait! I need to go back for a moment to say good-bye to my parents, but I want to follow you" (see 1 Kings 19:20).

Elijah responded, in effect, "Go on back. I'm not coming after you. If you don't come after me, you're going to miss your destiny, but I'm not going to beg you. I'm not going to coddle you into the Kingdom [pun intended]." God is saying to you and me, "I'm going to touch you with the anointing. If you don't respond, then the design will never become destiny."

Elisha made up his mind on the spot. He ran back and slew a yoke of oxen (see 1 Kings 19:21). Elisha's normal clothing, as the son of a rich farmer, was probably made out of pure silk. His decision to follow Elijah meant he would exchange his silk robes for robes made of animal hair (probably that of a ram or goat). These robes were probably uncomfortable and smelly, and they were generally worn by the lower classes of people. Yet God had made this lowly garment His mantle of anointing.

The Bible says Elisha slew his yoke of oxen and offered them as a sacrifice to God. Then he ran to minister to Elijah (see 1 Kings 19:21). He became Elijah's *sharath*, the man who "washed Elijah's hands," immersing himself in the vision of the reigning "king."

Too many people get a touch of God and instantly yield to the individualistic and egocentric ways of our culture. They immediately begin to think about, "My ministry...my work." Too many of us fail to realize we will only get "ours" through participation in "somebody else's." It may not work that way in the world, but that is the way it *always* works in the Kingdom of God.

Something marvelous happens when a man or a woman submits to God's pattern of training. The Bible says that David loved Saul greatly (see 1 Sam. 16:21). Now, Saul was not lovable—he had become a monster. Saul was awful because of the sin at work in him, but God gave David the ability to genuinely love Saul.

Love is not something you feel, it is something you do. You make up your mind, and "drive your love like a nail" into someone, and then the feelings will come. That's what happened to David. He said, "I'm going to love Saul." If you trace David's life through the Scriptures, you will find that David always called Saul by one title: *abba*. That means "my father." David loved the man who wanted to kill him.

I remember one particular day in my boyhood when I marched outside armed with a hammer and a large 20-penny nail. Now any time you give a child a hammer and a nail, you know he's going to tear up things. I decided to "fix" a tree in our backyard. After I finally got the nail started, I kept banging on that thing until I had beaten off all the bark on that poor tree. I was determined to drive that nail into the tree.

I went back to that place years later as a grown man and looked for that nail. I found it buried in the heart of the tree. After two decades of growth, the nail was covered so completely that you couldn't get it out without damaging the tree. God described David's love in Psalm 91:14: "Because he hath set his *love* upon Me, therefore will I deliver him: I will set him on high, because he hath known My name." The Hebrew word for "set one's love" in this passage is *cashaq*. It means "to drive your love like a nail" into someone. Evidently, David showed this same kind of love toward Saul—he drove his love into leadership.

I love to hear a young man or woman say, "This is my church, and this is my pastor. These are my elders. I'm here—sink or swim, live or die, come hell or high water." That's the stuff that leadership is made of.

The Bible also says David became Saul's "armour-bearer" (see 1 Sam. 16:21). Actually, David was Saul's armor bearer long before anyone ever made him Saul's "official" armor bearer. That's the way it should be. The Hebrew term for armor bearer is *nasa*. It means "to lift up." David was lifting up Saul. The word paints a picture of him getting his shoulders underneath to push up his leader.

Terry Nance says in his book, *God's Armorbearer*: "An armor bearer is one who carries his leader's shield into battle." He also said on page 35 of that nice little book, "His reason for being is the preservation of the life of the king."[1] He could have added, "...and the preservation of the leadership and effectiveness of the king."

This is the true scriptural pattern of leadership development. The Bible contains no such concept as a "Bible college" where you isolate yourself somewhere in a hot house and learn principles from all kinds of people. It speaks of certain "schools of the prophets" based right in a prophet's house, or based in the church of the prophet. The prophet would pour himself into his spiritual sons to create "sons of the prophets."

The Bible says, "For unto us a child is born, unto us a son is given" (Is. 9:6a). Children are born, but sons are *given*. One of the most powerful Greek words for "presented" is *paristemi*, which means "to take a stand alongside." Sons "imbibe the essence" of their father, and that's what David was trying to do, but Saul was unworthy. He never let David in. Who knows what would have happened if Saul had followed the pattern set by Moses in his relationship with Joshua? Everything Joshua became, he became through his apprenticeship to Moses. He got it by washing Moses' hands, by serving and watching his mentor. He literally walked in Moses' footsteps. No, he didn't look at Moses as God, but as God's chosen servant, and as a father. We have already examined the kind of relationship Elijah had with Elisha.

The twelve had this same relationship with Jesus. When Jesus called them, they dropped everything they

---

1. Terry Nance, *God's Armorbearer* (Tulsa, OK: Harrison House, Inc., 1990), p. 35.

were doing and followed Him. They recognized the hand of God in Jesus' call, and they left their businesses, their professions, their daily tasks, and their incomes—they left all those things at His word. You may be thinking, *Well, **that doesn't make any sense**.* I know, but the truth is that God will never lead you to do anything that is foolish in His eyes! Now those in the world will see things differently: God will often lead you to do things that seem foolish in the eyes of the world because He sees with a vision the world cannot have.

Jesus said, "For what shall it profit a man, if he shall gain the whole world, and lose his own soul?" (Mk. 8:36) What good is it if he gains the whole world and never determines or fulfills his destiny? I know the answer: It will all rot in his hands, and he will come to despise what he has spent his life accumulating. He will never have the joy of God flow up and out of his innermost being like rivers of living water (see Jn. 7:38).

I would rather live a day in my destiny than 100 years outside of it.

The late Watchman Nee reminds us that we will never have authority under us until we have established delegated authority over us." Isn't that powerful? Look at that again: *"You will never have authority under you until you have established delegated authority over you."* Brother Nee also said you should be able to write down the name of your delegated authority. Most people answer, "Well, God is my authority—G-O-D." No, that's rebellion talking. Who is the "delegated authority" God has placed in your life?

You are not merely receiving the person with the authority, you are receiving and honoring the "position of authority." When you "drive your love like a nail" into that person and position, God will take care of the rest. When the javelins fly—and they probably will since nobody is perfect—when your inheritance is stolen from you, your response will not be, "I'm going to get even!" or "I'm going to quit!" Your response will be, "Abba, Abba, I still love You." This is the real Bible college, the place of affliction-fired apprenticeship.

I believe this is the way Christian higher education will be accomplished in the next few years, because it goes back to biblical principles. At our Christian Life School of Theology headquartered in Columbus, Georgia, we brought together a faculty, an anointed curriculum, and everything else that is needed to train believers for reigning and for ministry. Now we bring it into local churches around the world, and place it into the hands of those respective apostolic authorities. These men and women of God are free to use it to mold their spiritual sons and daughters in God right there, in their local church setting. We believe that is the biblical pattern.

The first lesson David learned in Bethlehem was the lesson of spiritual authority. All of us have to learn this lesson before we can go on in God.

② The second lesson of Bethlehem is the lesson of *personal integrity*. David found a king to serve and came under spiritual authority. Then he found a giant to kill and came into personal integrity.

"And there went out a champion out of the camp of the Philistines, named Goliath, of Gath, whose height was six cubits and a span" (1 Sam. 17:4). A cubit was measured from a man's elbow to the tip of his longest finger. Goliath measured six cubits and a "span" in height. A span was the distance of an outstretched hand, measured from the thumb to the little finger—which was nearly always exactly half a cubit. In other words, Goliath was approximately nine-feet, two-inches tall! He was awesome, and he was a skilled warrior on top of everything else. The Bible calls Goliath the Philistine "champion" (the Hebrew root also means "middle man"), which means he was his nation's fighting representative. To become the champion, he had to be able to defeat everybody else in the army. David agreed to take on the fightingest Philistine of all the Philistines—who just happened to be nine-feet, two-inches tall.

The Bible describes other men who were larger than Goliath. One in particular measured nine-feet, six-inches tall, and he had six fingers on each hand, and six toes on each foot. He was a monster, but Goliath could whip him. *Goliath* is not a name; it is a title. It comes from the word *galah* which means "to behead ruthlessly." He was the "Terminator" of David's day. He was the "Number One Schwarzeneggar," the destroyer. This man could literally take your head off and take it off with a vengeance!

As soon as David decided to go for the gold of his destiny, Goliath came striding out onto the battlefield, saying, "Over my dead body." Now, every one of us has a Goliath lurking in the shadows of his life. Do you know what your Goliath is? You will meet your Goliath the moment you feel the touch of God's anointing. I can promise you that the moment you catch a glimpse of your destiny in God, your Goliath is going to rise up against you! Why? He knows that the only way for you to reach your destiny *is* "over his dead body." One of you must die for the other to live. If you reach your destiny, he will die. That is why your Goliath with stop you from achieving your destiny if he can! Don't kid yourself—you have a Goliath in the shadows of your life, and you'll never get out of Bethlehem without a fight.

Deal with Goliath in Bethlehem, in the early stages of your life. Fight your foe while you are still surrounded by your "family" in Christ. You are known and loved in Bethlehem. If you wait to meet your Goliath until you get down the road and start "waxing eloquent" on the things of God, people will already be expecting great things of you because they see you rightly dividing the word of truth. They see miracles start to flow in and out of your ministry, and they begin to place you on a special pedestal. The people around you will be expecting great things out of you.

If you haven't taken care of your Goliath in Bethlehem, then you will be attacked by him in a higher place where you will be embarrassed. Your family will be humiliated. The hundreds of people you have influenced for Christ will be devastated. *Deal with Goliath in Bethlehem!* Call him out of the shadows. Get him out in the brook, Kidron. Take a rock to his puffed-up head.

Do what David did—challenge and defeat your Goliath at "home" in the midst of family and friends! This is the place to do it. By "home," I mean your home church, your Bethlehem. The battlefield is the prayer room of your home church. Call out every hidden sin, every hidden hindrance, and every hidden enemy. Call those things up and out of you. Deal with them in Jesus' name. "Take their heads off" in Bethlehem, or they will destroy *you* later! The longer you leave your Goliath in there, the stronger he becomes, and the more vulnerable to him you become.

Goliath the champion, the beheader, wore a brass coat of mail that came down to his knees. For flexibility, it was made of interlocking rings that looked like fingernails or fish scales laid one on top of the other, and it was very heavy. His coat of mail weighed 148 pounds! The head of his spear weighed 17 pounds. Goliath was an awesome enemy.

Your own private Goliath may look just as frightening to you. Whatever that Goliath is, I tell you that you can handle it in Bethlehem! What "strongman" is shouting at you from the shadows of your mind? What stronghold stands between you and your dream from God? What vain and taunting imagination needs to be cast down in your life?

This is the Goliath that we need to deal with in Bethlehem. There are several kinds of Goliaths; some are internal, others are external. The "internal Goliaths" fall into three categories. Although we will look closely at these "Goliaths" later on, I want to mention them to you now. The first group of "Goliaths" are demon spirits. The second Goliath rises up from our carnal nature. The third Goliath often wears church clothes, because he is called "tradition."

Internal Goliaths desperately want to "take the head off your dream" so they can destroy the divine destiny of your life. The external Goliaths include "family" members. David's own brothers rose up against him with bitter anger, as did Joseph's brothers.

The second external Goliath we face is the temptation to substitute the world's (or enemy's) methods for God's methods. We have found it "easy" over these years to "do the work of the Kingdom" with worldly methodologies and motives. "If I can just have a little bit more money and a little bit bigger this or better that...."

No matter where you are in your walk with God, you must never avoid or forget the lessons of Bethlehem. God is taking you from glory to glory as He conforms you to the image of His Son—and He expects you to retain the foundations He lays at each stage. Now it is time to face your Goliath in Bethlehem.

Chapter 2

Battle for Integrity

Once David found a king to serve and learned the lesson of spiritual authority in Bethlehem, he had to learn a second lesson in the "House of Bread," the lesson of *personal integrity*. He found a giant to kill, for that is the *only way* to learn personal integrity.

The word "integrity" comes from the root word *integer*. It literally means to be the same thing on the outside that you are on the inside, and vice versa. It means to be of one essence. You "have integrity" when you become one, integrated, an integer.

David had to learn this, and so do you and I. Yet most Christians live schizophrenic or split-minded lives, serving God on Sunday, immersing themselves in the world's entanglements on Saturday, and virtually bowing to the devil Monday through Friday! This is a sure prescription for trouble. God's Word declares, "A double-minded man is unstable in all his ways" (Jas. 1:8). A "schizophrenic believer" is fragmented and diluted in mind and heart.

If you try to "play both ends against the middle" by sandwiching your Sunday morning Christianity between the world and the devil, then the enemy's demons are going to pick you apart as though you were a carcass. They will leave nothing behind but dry bones. In total contrast, the Bible declares:

> *Put on the whole armour of God, that ye may be able to stand against the wiles of the devil. For we wrestle not against flesh and blood, but against principalities, against powers, against the rulers of the darkness of this world, against spiritual wickedness in high places. Wherefore take unto you the whole armour of God, that ye may be able to withstand in the evil day, and having done all, to stand* (Ephesians 6:11-13).

Very often, demon spirits get a foothold or establish a stronghold in a human life during the first seven years of a child's life due to abuse of various kinds. These spirits also assault humans through "imaginations." The Greek for "imaginations" is *dialogismos*, which is similar to *dialogos* and *dialogia*, the Greek roots of "dialogue." The enemy uses imaginations to set up an "internal dialogue" so that you will respond in a certain way when certain things occur. His goal is to block the expression of your divine inner design from coming into fruition.

Paul said these "imaginations" are high places that must be cast down (see 2 Cor. 10:5). The Greek prefix *dia* means "through," and *logia* means "word." For example, men become convinced they must act a certain way when a female form walks by. Something has been "set up" that needs to be dealt with.

Job declared, "I made a covenant with mine eyes" in Job 31:1. You have to cut a covenant to bring out vain imaginations and reveal demons. Pull those things down and allow God's divine design to flow through your life at all times. Madison Avenue sells everything on the basis of vain imaginations and carnal appetites. Our media is set up to "feed these imaginations" all the time. They must be brought down, and the apostle Paul told us how to do it:

(For the weapons of our warfare are not carnal, but mighty through God to the pulling down of strong holds;) casting down imaginations [dialogia], and every high thing that exalteth itself against the knowledge of God, and bringing into captivity every thought to the obedience of Christ (2 Corinthians 10:4-5).

Ungodly thought patterns, stimulus responses, and spiritual bonds—they all have to be undone. How can you do that? How do you deal with demons? Jesus and the apostles showed us that we have to cast out demons. Sometimes you can't do it with just a touch. You have to have some understanding of what is being dissolved, torn down, uprooted, and cut out by the Holy Spirit. Paul assures us the Word of the living God can do it.

For the word of God is quick, and powerful, and sharper than any twoedged sword, piercing even to the dividing asunder of soul and spirit, and of the joints and marrow, and is a discerner of the thoughts and intents of the heart (Hebrews 4:12).

The Greek word for "quick" is the word *zao*. Do you know what that means? It means the "life of God." The writer is saying, "The word [the *logos*] of God is alive with divine life!" The Greek word for "powerful" in this verse is *energe*. It means "energetic, full of divine energy." God's Word is quick and powerful, and sharper than any surgeon's scalpel (or two-edged sword). It is so sharp that it easily "parts the flesh" so that you can get down to the *dialogia*. It pierces the flesh to the "dividing asunder of soul and spirit, and joints and marrow." Marrow is the blood bank in the center of the bones that feeds the body with blood through the joints. The joints don't generate the blood; it comes from the bone marrow.

The Word of God can divide the very thoughts and intents of heart, as well as reveal the deepest motivations of our lives. We need to bathe ourselves in the Book and keep ourselves in God's living Word because it has the life and the power we need to cast down every evil imagination.

The second kind of Goliath is really worse than demon spirits—it is our carnal nature. The carnal nature is tougher to deal with than demon spirits because you can cast out demon spirits, but you have to crucify the carnal nature. Crucifixion is more painful than "casting out." Paul told the believers in Rome, "For the good that I would I do not: but the evil which I would not, that I do" (Rom. 7:19).

When I was younger, I didn't want to read that verse because I didn't want to believe that the great apostle Paul ever did evil. Then I discovered that the Greek word for "evil" used in this verse is not the usual *poneros*, which means "malicious, vicious, wicked, and malevolent." Paul said, "the *kakos* which I would not, that I do." Paul was merely acknowledging that he had some *kakos* too, just like us. Sometimes he missed the mark a little bit, because even the apostle Paul battled his carnal nature.

One time I was praying about something after I had mistreated somebody. I had done something ugly—I had "*kaka*'ed" somebody. I knelt down and I said, "Lord, help me with this problem. I don't want to be like that. Cast this ugly disposition out of me." Then He said, "It's not something you can cast out, son. You have to nail that thing to the tree. It's something *you* have to do." He told me, "I have already taken care of it—now you have to appropriate what I have done in your own personal life. It's going to be hard, but you have to do it. Just go back there and ask for forgiveness."

"Confess your faults one to another, and pray one for another, that ye may be healed" (Jas. 5:16a). Ask for forgiveness, admit that you're a scoundrel and a skunk. Admit that you've done some bad things and ask for forgiveness. Make up your mind to go the other way. Break the cycle of habit and carnality. You might be thinking, *Yeah, but that's embarrassing! It hurts my ego.* That's right—it's time for a crucifixion. You have to get on that tree!

The third internal Goliath, the monster that causes so much damage in the Body of Christ, is the Goliath of tradition. What are "the seven last words of the Church"? Do these sound familiar? "But we've always done it that way."

"But we've always done it that way!" You can be bound by tradition just as surely as those grave clothes held back Lazarus in the tomb of death. Yet Jesus has a better plan for you, just as He did for Lazarus. You have to be willing to go a new direction if that is the way Jesus is going!

Paul wrote these fabulous words in Ephesians 5:14: "Wherefore He saith, Awake thou that sleepest, and arise from the dead...." He isn't talking about physical death here; he uses the Greek word *nekros*, which means "spiritual slumber." God wants us to rise out of our spiritual slumber; then Christ will give us light.

You may face some "external Goliaths" too. Remember that a Goliath is a beheader who can take the head right off your destiny. Yet Jesus declared, "...I give unto them [you and me] eternal life; and they shall never perish, neither shall any man pluck them out of My hand" (Jn. 10:28). There isn't a single created thing or spirit that can take your destiny away from you—except for one person: you. Unfortunately, that Goliath inside you can cause you to do something destructive if you don't deal with it.

External "Goliaths" also need to be dealt with. The first "Goliath" David faced wasn't standing in the valley— he was dressed as a soldier in Saul's army, and he had a very familiar voice—he was Eliab, David's oldest brother! Hostile family members are often transformed into Goliaths that ruthlessly behead and kill your destiny.

When Samuel went to Bethlehem to anoint Israel's new king from among Jesse's sons, the first son to stand before him was Eliab. Now the arrival of this feared prophet wasn't a surprise; everyone knew when he arrived. Eliab had obviously been preparing and waiting for the moment he was called before the prophet. He thought, *Surely I'm the one, because I'm the crown prince; I'm the elder brother of my father's house.*

Eliab wasn't the only one thinking he was "the one." Samuel thought the same thing! He thought, *Wow, this is the man. Boy, look at him! He's an image. Just look at him—he's tremendous. He even looks like a king.* That was until God stepped in and said, "Don't look on the outward appearance. I look on the heart" (see 1 Sam. 16:5-7).

There was something wrong with Eliab's heart. Now you will see what that flaw was. After this elder brother was publicly passed over, you can imagine how his hatred for David grew. He already had a predisposition to despise his youngest and "most insignificant" brother. There is evidence that David might have been only the half-brother of Eliab and the others. In fact, he might have been illegitimate! When David showed up at the battlefront with some supplies from their father, Jesse, that was "the last straw." Eliab said, "Why did you come down here?"

And David spake to the men that stood by him, saying, What shall be done to the man that killeth this Philistine, and taketh away the reproach from Israel? for who is this uncircumcised Philistine, that he should defy the armies of the living God? ... And Eliab his eldest brother heard when he spake unto the men; and Eliab's anger was kindled against David, and he said, Why camest thou down hither? and with whom hast thou left those few sheep in the wilderness? I know thy pride, and the naughtiness of thine heart; for thou art come down that thou mightest see the battle (1 Samuel 17:26,28).

I imagine David watched over a very large flock of sheep, since Jesse had all those sons he could give for military service—he was probably a man of great wealth and means. When Eliab scornfully said, "I know thy pride and the *naughtiness* of thine heart," he used the Hebrew word *ra*. He was telling David, "I know what is in you. You are inferior, useless, and spoiled. I'm on to your tricks...." Doesn't that sound like a big brother? "Who do you think you are? Cool it kid. Why, I knew you when you were only...you just came down here to see the battle." Doesn't that sound like a member of the family talking?

Jesse told his youngest son, "I want you to find out what's going on with your brothers in the war. Then come back and tell us all about it" (see 1 Sam. 17:17-18). When David arrived at the front line, he heard Goliath bellowing out blasphemies against God and Israel. He was so upset about it that once he delivered his goods into the right hands he began looking for his brothers to find out why this man wasn't being challenged! All he got for his trouble was scorn and ridicule from his own kin.

David was facing a "Goliath" even before he gathered up the smooth stones for a battle with the man shouting in the valley: His own family members were trying to remove the head from his destiny.

David's answer to Eliab's challenge before he met Goliath sets a precedent for us today:

And David said, What have I now done? Is there not a cause? And he turned from him toward another, and spake after the same manner... (1 Samuel 17:29-30).

He was basically telling his brother, "Haven't I already accomplished what I am now proposing to do? Do you remember the bear and the lion? Is there not a cause?" I love the Hebrew word David used here. *Davar* has the same meaning as the Greek word *logos*. Both of these words refer to "principles." David was saying, "Is there not a *word* from God? Is there not a *principle* here?" David was saying, "This man is cursing and blaspheming God! Why are all of you sitting around shaking in your boots and allowing this blasphemy to go forth over Israel? It's a matter of principle!" This must be your answer to family members and friends who say, "We know you—why you will never amount to anything! How dare you try to be different from us!"

David was 20-21 years old at this time, which was about five years after Samuel anointed him in front of his brothers. Don't think of him as a 17-year-old boy—that's just preaching, not teaching. He is a grown man, with every right to go out there, even though he was still a "youth" with no formal training as a soldier.

David was angry and he had a right to be. He asked Eliab, "Is there not a command, a promise, a word, a principle at stake here?" David broke a time-honored family tradition when he defied and questioned his brother; because in that culture, the eldest brother was treated with the same honor as a father by all of his younger brothers and sisters. He was the "crown prince" and "heir apparent" of the family. However, David was motivated by a higher law, a deeper truth, and a more vital principle, or word, from God; in his fear and intimidation, Eliab had allowed a divine principle to go unanswered.

When David stepped forward, he incited Eliab's anger because he had come against Eliab's authority and personal honor by refusing to join him in his cowardice. David had other reasons to fight Goliath as well as principle. The Bible says,

> *And the men of Israel said, Have ye seen this man that is come up? surely to defy Israel is he come up: and it shall be, that the man who killeth him, the king will enrich him with great riches, and will give him his daughter, and make his father's house free in Israel* (1 Samuel 17:25).

David didn't fight Goliath for nothing.

You and I don't serve God for nothing! You are probably thinking right now, "Wait a minute—of course we serve God for nothing!" No, we get *everything* when we serve God! If you're still saying, "But I don't want anything!" then you're crazy. You should want everything God has! First of all, you should want it because God wants you to! Some people say, "Why I never give so that I can get." Well I do it every day. Every time I give, I want to get more so I can give more! That is the true biblical principle of prosperity.

For too many years we have moped around saying, "I want to stay humble and poor so I can be holy." I don't have to be poor to be holy. King Saul promised to enrich any champion of Israel with great riches, along with the hand of his daughter in marriage. That means the king would make the winner a "member of the family." Finally, the king promised any would-be champion that his father's house would be declared "free in Israel," which meant no more taxation, a "friend of the King."

First, there was the divine principle of God. Second, there was the king's personal promise of reward.

David ran into another Goliath, a very subtle Goliath, when he was called to stand before King Saul. The next attack on his destiny came right down from apostolic authority, from the king himself!

And David said to Saul, Let no man's heart fail because of him; thy servant will go and fight with this Philistine. And Saul said to David, Thou art not able to go against this Philistine to fight with him: for thou art but a youth, and he a man of war from his youth (1 Samuel 17:32-33).

David met this "beheading" statement with an even more powerful word of testimony to God's faithfulness. After he told Saul about killing a marauding lion and a bear with his bare hands when they attacked his sheep, he told the astonished king:

Thy servant slew both the lion and the bear: and this uncircumcised Philistine shall be as one of them, seeing he hath defied the armies of the living God. David said moreover, The Lord that delivered me out of the paw of the lion, and out of the paw of the bear, He will deliver me out of the hand of this Philistine. And Saul said unto David, Go, and the Lord be with thee (1 Samuel 17:36-37).

Saul remembered enough about the miracles God had done in his own past to think, *This kid's just crazy enough to pull this off. This thing just might happen.*

Saul basically told David, "Now, David, you can't fight this Goliath without some help. So let me tell you how to do it, son." Then he gave David his own armor to wear. David must have been a pretty good-sized guy if this six-foot, eight-inch tall king thought his armor would fit David. Forget the Sunday school pictures: David was no shrimp.

The Bible says, "And David girded his sword upon his armour, and he *assayed* to go; for he had not proved it. And David said unto Saul, I cannot go with these; for I have not proved them. And David put them off him" (1 Sam. 17:39). The Scriptures say David "assayed" to go. The word *assay* in the Hebrew means about what it meant in the old western movies! The goldminers in California always took their ore to the *assayer* in the *assay house* where the ore was tested and weighed to determine if it was real gold or fool's gold. *Assay* means "to weigh out." So David "weighed out" Saul's armor and asked himself, "Now, shall I fight with this armor or not?"

Most of us picture David stumbling around in big over-sized armor, but the truth is that we really don't know how big David was. However, given Saul's offer to lend his armor to David, he must have been close to Saul's size. The armor probably was workable, but *it wasn't David's!*

David *assayed* or weighed out that armor and said, "I cannot go with these; for I have not proved them." He had never tested them in battle, and he wasn't sure those methods would work. He "put them off him" and turned to the proven weapons and methods God had provided in the wilderness. We need to learn something from this episode:

You can learn principles and character from the reigning king, but you must learn to fight the warfare of faith for yourself.

I can't pray your prayers for you. You don't want my armor because it is my armor. You need to have your own armor. You can learn principles from me, but don't try to learn techniques.

One of my teachers in Florida laughed at himself in class one day and said, "I remember when I was young, my pastor parted his hair in a certain way; and he wore a certain kind of shoe, along with a certain kind of tie and shirt." He smiled and admitted, "I found myself parting my hair just like him. In fact, I even wore the same shoes, shirts, and ties. That was wrong. That is not becoming a son."

David learned to fight God's battles God's way while he was in the wilderness. He decided to "stick with a winner." The Bible says, "And he took his staff in his hand, and chose him five smooth stones out of the brook" (1 Sam. 17:40a). The Hebrew word *nachal* is translated "brook" in this passage, but it actually means "out of the valley."

If you go to Israel, you will discover that this location was literally the whole Kidron valley—that is where these two opposing armies had gathered. So David gathered smooth stones "out of the Kidron valley." Yes, there is a Kidron brook, but the important point is that David was standing on the ancient battle ground of the Kidron Valley. You can walk anywhere in that valley, and pick almost any spot to sit down, and still pick up 50 to 100 stones.

David laid aside Saul's bulky armor, the man-made instrument of defense. Instead, he selected the offensive weapons God had given him, the weapons he had personally proven in the heat of conflict. He just picked up five smooth stones for his shepherd's sling and put them in his bag before he came against Goliath. As he declared in his psalms, his God was his "buckler and shield" (see Ps. 91:4).

Look closely at what Goliath said to David: "And the Philistine said to David, Come to me, and I will give thy flesh unto the fowls of the air, and to the beasts of the field" (1 Sam. 17:44).

David's encounter with Goliath reveals a crucial spiritual principle. *Every one of us has a Goliath!* Each Goliath has the power, and indeed exists for the purpose of "feeding our flesh to the fowls of the air and the beasts of the field." Whenever you see the Hebrew word *Ba'al Zebuwb* (transliterated as "Beelzebub" in the Authorized Version), in the Old Testament, or the English translation, "Lord of the flies" or "Lord of dung" applied to a winged creature, know that this passage is not referring to an eagle, a raven, or a dove—this is a demon spirit.

Goliath said, "David, come to me, and I'm going to feed your *basar*, your flesh...." Goliath was talking about more than David's physical body; he was talking about his flesh nature, his carnal nature. "You just come to me, David, and I'm going to feed your prideful, carnal nature to the demon spirits and to the *behemah*, or the 'beasts' of the field." Since Goliath was threatening to feed David's carnal flesh to "flesh-eaters," it is my personal belief that the generic "dumb beast" word actually refers to jackals (*ze'eb*), the carnivorous carrion-eaters that run and hunt in packs. Jackals or wolves are a second major metaphor or illustration of demon spirits in the Bible.

In the flesh or carnal realm, Goliath has every right to destroy and consume carnal flesh. If David had come against Goliath in his own pride or fleshly nature, Goliath would have slaughtered him. Goliath would have lifted his body up on the point of that massive spear so the demon spirits of the air could pick his carcass clean.

I've seen too much preaching and so-called "ministry" in the flesh! Do you know what happens? It draws the wrong kind of crowd—it sparks a feeding frenzy among flesh-feeding demons! They feed on the carnal flesh nature of mankind. The more flesh you have, the more demons you draw! The less flesh in any place, the less demons gather in that place. That should serve as a solemn warning to ministers who like to parade and charade in their flesh nature. Jesus warned the boldest of His disciples:

...Simon, Simon, behold, Satan hath desired to have you, that he may sift you as wheat: but I have prayed for thee, that thy faith fail not: and when thou art converted, strengthen thy brethren (Luke 22:31-32).

Peter may have thought, *Pray for me? Forget that jazz! Get a hold of that devil and get him out of here. I mean, You can do it!* I believe Jesus would have said, "No, I'm going to pray for you. You don't know it, but satan exists so that he can destroy your flesh." If you become one with your flesh, then you will learn firsthand what hell is all about! The worst horrors of hell involve the devil destroying what he can destroy—forever. Hell on earth arrives whenever you lose your spiritual identity in your carnal nature. There simply isn't a better description of hell.

If you and I fight in the spirit, Goliath's demons will go hungry, and we will win. On the other hand, if we go out in our own fleshly, carnal nature, we will become a feast for the carnivores of the air because demon spirits feed on the carrion of our carnal human nature. The feast begins when by walking in the flesh we allow "Goliath the beheader" to lop off the head of our destiny in Christ.

When David knocked Goliath down with a stone from his sling, he didn't stop there. He literally removed Goliath's head from his shoulders with the giant's own sword. *You can't leave your Goliath with his head on either!* You have to take his head off. David didn't delay or avoid his confrontation with his Goliath; he called him out in Bethlehem and ran to meet him in battle.

You may be afraid of being embarrassed or of failing, but it's better to be embarrassed at home in Bethlehem than to be destroyed or humiliated later on in Zion. Whatever your personal "Goliath" is, you need to "call him out" while you are surrounded by friends and family on your home turf.

Chapter 3

The Search
for Sexual Intimacy

David's third lesson in Bethlehem didn't go very well. First he learned about spiritual authority by "finding a king to serve." He submitted himself to God's established authority. Then he learned about personal integrity by "finding a giant to kill." He discovered and confirmed his true identity through defeating a force determined to behead his destiny in God.

Now David had to learn about *sexual intimacy* in Bethlehem. This is a lesson David did not learn well. This unlearned lesson became David's "Achilles' heel" or vulnerable spot for the rest of his life. He just couldn't seem to say "no" to a pretty face or a beautiful form. He wanted to possess nearly every woman that came across his path. David's failure began with Saul's broken covenant.

*And the men of Israel said, Have ye seen this man that is come up? surely to defy Israel is he come up: and it shall be, that the man who killeth him, the king will enrich him with **great riches**, and will **give him his daughter**, and make his **father's house free** in Israel* (1 Samuel 17:25).

The second part of that verse fascinates me. God intended for Merab, Saul's elder daughter, to be David's wife and life partner. Merab's name literally means "increase." It means "to be cast together in a fine manner, to become or be many more." She was quite a lady, and she was the exact mate David needed—a marvelous woman who could give birth to many, many sons and daughters. David needed that kind of life partner to help him build a kingdom.

And Saul said to David, Behold my elder daughter Merab, her will I give thee to wife: only be thou valiant for me, and fight the Lord's battles. For Saul said, Let not mine hand be upon him, but let the hand of the Philistines be upon him. And David said unto Saul, Who am I? and what is my life, or my father's family in Israel, that I should be son-in-law to the king? But it came to pass at the time when Merab Saul's daughter should have been given to David, that she was given unto Adriel the Meholathite to wife (1 Samuel 18:17-19).

Saul promised David, "I'll give you Merab if you will go out there and destroy these Philistines for me." Yet he hated David so much that he was hoping the Philistines would kill him in battle. The greatest affront came in verse 19, which says, "But it came to pass at the time when Merab Saul's daughter should have been given to David, that she was given unto Adriel the Meholathite to wife."

Saul stole David's rightful inheritance although he had defeated Goliath and battled the Philistines as the captain of a thousand men for the right to marry Merab. David fought Goliath to honor God; but he also wanted to be made rich, marry Merab and become a member of the king's household, and see his father's house declared "free in all of Israel."

This was David's rightful inheritance on the force of the king's spoken word. Yet when the time came for Merab to become David's wife, Saul took her and maliciously gave her to another man, totally violating his given word.

Who was this other man? *Adriel* means "power, ample, or rich." So *Merab*, "increase," was given to *Adriel*, "Mr. Rich." Saul wanted a relationship of convenience and political alliance with this man, so he casually violated his solemn word and gave his daughter to this rich man. How did this man make his money? Again, the key to the man is found in his name. Adriel was the son of *Barzillai*, the *Meholathite*.

Meholathite means "to round dance, to twirl." Its primary root word is *kheel*, which is also used to describe "whirling Dervishes," the Moslem ascetics who whirl and dance in their religious rites. *Kheel* was used to describe Elijah the prophet when he was under the anointing. Adriel's people were wild dancers who whirled and twisted in contorted dancing. Some scholars say they had a right to be wildly ecstatic because they were rich: *Barzillai* means "son of iron."

Saul gave his daughter to a man from a family of iron workers. They probably had a liaison with the Philistines, which makes them immediately suspect in my mind! Evidently, that didn't bother Saul one iota. This tribe or family had the ability or Philistine permission to work in metal despite the general ban on Israelites possessing metal that the Philistines enforced when they could. Saul probably got his armor through Adriel, the Meholathite!

Once again, it appears Saul was thinking like a worldling: *I've got to forge an alliance with this traitor family of metalworkers so I can keep the metal coming in. I need to keep the swords, chariots, and armor coming in.* He gave away David's inheritance to secure his own lifestyle and wishes, and he did it without hesitation.

The Church doesn't always do everything right. Even Christian leaders will take matters into their own hands at times and end up robbing you of your inheritance. David was robbed of his inheritance because of a worldly, unspiritual leader. It will probably happen to you one day if it hasn't happened already.

If it happens and you throw up your hands and quit, who gets hurt in the end? You do. How did David deal with the loss of his inheritance, and how did he make the most of his failures? The answers to these questions could be the key to your success in the Kingdom of God!

David found a friend to love in Jonathan, who stood by him although Saul robbed David of Merab and the rest of his inheritance. Saul's sin ultimately robbed him of Jonathan's friendship as well when father and son were killed in a misbegotten battle with the Philistines—separated from God's help and protection by Saul's stubborn sin. (By the way, don't believe the garbage generated about Jonathan's relationship with David. The myth that David and Jonathan had a homosexual relationship was concocted by certain pseudo-scholars who don't even know the Lord, let alone His living Word.) If anything, David was *too interested* in women!

Saul didn't treat David right, and people in the Church won't always treat us right either. The only problem with the Church is that it is made up of human beings who are frail and faulty.

Saul broke his word and gave Merab to a rich traitor for political gain. But when David wasn't killed in his battles with the Philistines as Saul had hoped, he came up with another scheme to salvage what was left of his name—and destroy his young enemy.

And Michal Saul's daughter loved David: and they told Saul, and the thing pleased him. And Saul said, I will give him her, that she may be a snare to him, and that the hand of the Philistines may be against him. Wherefore Saul said to David, Thou shalt this day be my son-in-law in the one of the twain (1 Samuel 18:20-21).

Michal is an enigma. She seems to be one thing while actually being and doing something hidden from casual observation. She ran to Papa Saul after he married Merab off to Adriel and told her daddy that she "loved" David. She was Daddy's younger daughter, and evidently she was incapable of loving anybody but herself. When she said she "loved" David, the Bible uses the Hebrew word *ahav*.

Do you remember King Ahab, Jezebel's husband? His name in Hebrew is *Ahav* or *Ahab*. Ahab the "lover" was actually a lover of "himself." Michal was a female version of Jezebel's husband. She came to Saul and said, "Daddy, Daddy, I want David. I want David!" She liked the way David looked and handled himself. She saw David in uniform and fell "head over heels"—infatuated with him.

Michal desired and coveted David as a possession. The bottom line is that she had a strong, emotional attachment and desire to *possess* David (that's the meaning of *ahav*. It is near in meaning to the Greek *eros* or even *epithumia* [lust]). Saul said, "I will give him her, that she may be a *snare* to him" (1 Sam. 18:21). Michal is fascinating to me.

Her name means "a shallow brook." What kind of noise does a shallow brook make? It babbles. How would you like to go to sleep every night with a babbler on the pillow beside you? All she did was talk, talk, talk, and talk: She was a babbler, a babbling brook with no depth. She must have been totally different from Merab in personality and character.

Saul thought, *Ah-ha. This is exactly what he needs. The Philistines couldn't kill him, and Goliath couldn't kill him, but I've got a daughter who can!* Do you realize that Michal came closer to destroying David than anyone or anything else in David's life—with the possible exception of Bath-sheba? She shut him out. She failed or absolutely refused to provide the sexual intimacy, soul companionship, and partnership that David needed. *Everybody* needs these things, and every married person is entitled to receive them from his or her mate. Michal fulfilled her father's hopes when she became a "snare" to David instead of a helpmeet. The Hebrew word for "snare" is *moqesh*. It means "a trap, a noose around the neck, a scandal, a snare." It has about the same meaning as the Greek word *skandalon*. Largely thanks to Michal, her marriage to David became a scandal, an elaborate snare of the enemy for the man after God's own heart.

This snare marked the greatest area of failure in David's lifetime. Can you see why? It wasn't totally David's fault, although David contributed to it himself in a great many ways. What did God do about it? He gave David a true friend in Jonathan. David had Merab as a promise; he got Michal as its empty fulfillment; and in the end, God helped fill his hollow yearning with the true friendship of a public figure, both women's famous brother, Jonathan.

After Saul gave Merab to "Old Money Bags" Adriel, she bore Adriel five sons and then died. We don't know if there were daughters involved, because no children are mentioned other than her five sons. Can you see what I was saying about this lady named "increase"? David needed her, along with all those sons and the daughters she probably bore as well. Perhaps she would have lived longer in David's anointed household.

As for Michal, she left David when he went into Adullam. She stayed home with Papa Saul because she wasn't going to live in any cave—after all, she had been brought up a princess in the royal house. Her inner character again rose to the surface seven years later, the day David tucked up his garment like a slave and tied it around him so he could dance without hindrance before the Lord as the ark of the covenant was returned to Israel.

Michal looked down her long blue-blood nose and sniffed, "I don't want anything to do with that, David. You made a fool out of both of us today" (see 2 Sam. 6:16-23). This is an accurate picture of the kind of person she was. Like her man-fearing father, Michal was very unspiritual; and it was a costly error. The Bible says she was barren from that time on (see 2 Sam. 6:23). She remained barren even after Saul "removed" her from David's house and "gave" her to another man as his wife.

Second Samuel 21:8 says something very odd about this barren ex-wife of David: "But the king took the two sons of Rizpah the daughter of Aiah, whom she bare unto Saul, Armoni and Mephibosheth; and the *five sons of Michal*...." If Michal was barren, how could she have five sons? Keep on reading: "...the five sons of Michal the daughter of Saul, whom she brought up for Adriel the son of Barzillai the Meholathite."

When Merab died, Michal obviously went to the home of Adriel to care for his children. That wouldn't have bothered Saul at all. Those five young princes were important to the kingdom because Michal, his only other daughter, was barren. There might even have been a crown prince among those sons of Merab. So Michal reared the five boys in the home of Adriel, the son of Barzillai the Meholathite.

The striking conclusion to the story of Merab's sons is the fact that all five sons were slaughtered in the end. Because Saul had rashly broken a covenant and by trying to wipe out the Gibeonites to please the people, God lifted His blessings from the land and a three-year drought set in. The Bible says the Lord lifted the curse over the land after the five sons of Merab and two sons of Saul by Rizpah the concubine were turned over to the Gibeonites (see 2 Sam. 21:1-9). The Gibeonites executed all seven men at once on a mass gallows, and hung their bodies on the walls of Bethshan. (I've stood there by the wall of Bethshan, and I've looked at the place where those bodies were displayed.)

What a tragedy. Do you see what Saul did to himself and his family when he came against David, the man of God, and stole his inheritance from him? Saul literally wiped out his own lineage in the kingdom! Don't ever raise your hand or tongue against God's anointed. Let God take care of wrongs done. Yes, people will do wrong to you and hurt you, but God will deal with that. Don't take vengeance into your own hands.

Saul literally wiped out his own posterity through his rebellion and disobedience. Jonathan and another son died with Saul, leaving only Ishbosheth, Saul's renegade son who worshipped Ba'al and Jonathan's crippled son, Mephibosheth, whom David spared.

David did absolutely nothing when Saul stole his inheritance from him. He did not raise his hands to grasp what was his, nor did he get angry. He did not fight or curse Saul. He just let it go and put his trust in the Lord. But God didn't let it go. No, God took care of this injustice personally.

What about the man God gave to David as a friend? Six years or so before David fought Goliath, Jonathan had already become a national hero in Israel! He and his armor bearer made a daring raid behind enemy lines into a large camp of fully armed Philistine soldiers. Jonathan rushed into the camp swinging swords and lopping off heads. When the dust settled, Jonathan had single-handedly slaughtered 20 Philistine warriors, and sent the whole company or battalion of Philistines scampering down the mountainside for their lives, which in turn caused several thousand Philistine soldiers nearby to scatter and flee in fear (see 1 Sam. 14:12-20).

So Jonathan was at least six years older than David, and Jonathan was no wimp. He could have worn those royal robes of Saul just as well as David, except for one important thing. Jonathan was the kind of man who believed God more than anyone else.

Jonathan heard that God had anointed David as king of Israel. He himself was in line for that position, but the day came when he took off his royal robe and laid it at David's feet. He said, "I know this belongs to you, not to me." And they loved each other. Their hearts were knitted together by the Spirit of God so thoroughly that Jonathan repeatedly defied his own father and king to save David's life.

When Jonathan was killed with his father at the battle of Mount Gilboa, David lifted up his voice and cried, "I am distressed for thee, my brother Jonathan: very pleasant hast thou been unto me: thy love to me was wonderful, passing the love of women" (2 Sam. 1:26). Now the King James Version says "women," but I believe David was saying "wives." He was crying out from the depths of his own painful experience with Michal, the babbler, the scornful snare, the withholder of affection, trust, and intimacy. "I found the love in you, Jonathan, that I didn't find in the daughters of Saul. God gave it to me in you, Jonathan."

If you are unmarried but carry a desire for a mate, God has somebody for you. He has your David or Merab waiting in the wings, but you have to find that special someone in Bethlehem. Find your mate in the Body of Christ, not out in the world. God has a special person for you unless He has called and anointed you for singleness. (You'll know it if that is the case.) Whatever your situation may be, put your faith and trust in God. He has that person for you.

This problem with intimacy plagued David throughout his life because he did not find what he needed in the beginning. I don't want to blame anybody else, because David is culpable here. When David finally came to Zion as king of Israel, he took more concubines and wives out of Jerusalem (see 2 Sam. 5:13). David had everything. He was the king, and he was a "man after the heart of God."

In fact, he already had several wives with excellent qualities—especially Abigail the Carmelitess, the widow of Nabal. Why couldn't he resist a pretty face and an attractive form? He failed again and again in this area.

This particular "Goliath" rose up again in Second Samuel chapter 11, when from a nearby rooftop David saw Bathsheba bathing. He didn't turn away and "flee youthful lusts." No, his eyes focused right there. He got into deep trouble and committed adultery with her. When Bathsheba became pregnant, David actually had her husband killed with the collusion of Joab, his nephew and the captain of his army. David never mastered this problem of intimacy in Bethlehem, and it brought disaster in Zion and became the greatest "Achilles' heel" in his life!

Learn this lesson well if you want to be a servant of the King. Don't minimize this problem. Every minister must come to grips with his or her sexuality. We must all find a godly way to meet our needs in this area—and we must do it in Bethlehem.

Young men often start their search for their Merab by looking first for outward beauty. They look for somebody who has flesh or sex appeal. (I'm just telling it like it is.) It isn't right, and it isn't good—in fact, it's stupid—but this is the way many men operate.

The second thing young men look for is the capability of friendship. Does she have a pleasant personality? This is the area of the soul. Is she bright and witty? Can she hold her own in an adult conversation? Is she somebody I will be proud of?

Last of all, and lowest on the priority list, they look for partnership, because this is the area of the spirit. This is unfortunate because we all really need somebody who is going to stand with us through all of the "ups and downs" of life. We all need someone who understands us, cares about us, and is willing to "get in the harness" with us to make our lives work. This aspect of the spiritual character within should carry 70 percent of the weight, while the soulish attributes should amount to about 20 percent, leaving the passing physical attributes about 10 percent of the "importance factor" in choosing a mate.

Wise men and most women look for a partner who knows and loves them first. They look for someone they can "hook up" with at a deeper, spiritual level. Then they look for friendship, and lastly they look for intimacy or sex appeal. (They know that intimacy will automatically spring up where the other factors are present.)

And if I could give one word of advice to young men in the Kingdom of God, it would be this: Look at the inner person when you're searching for a mate. Physical appearance contributes only a fraction to what makes someone beautiful. Beauty is mostly rooted in the spiritual person. True and lasting beauty comes from the inside.

Once we learn the lessons of Bethlehem about spiritual authority, personal integrity, and sexual intimacy, we can move on to the lessons of the next classroom. Unfortunately, most of us spend too much time saying, "Oh, God, get me out of here. Get me out of Bethlehem. Why did this happen to me?" God has to keep on saying, "Learn the lessons; learn the lessons now so you won't have to relearn them later." If you and I will focus on learning the lessons of Bethlehem, then God can focus on moving us on up and out to the "next classroom."

Part II

Adullam—Dangling at the End of the Rope

The Place of Testing, Learning, and Growing

Chapter 4

Compassion From the Cave Adullam

David therefore departed thence, and escaped to the cave Adullam: and when his brethren and all his father's house heard it, they went down thither to him (1 Samuel 22:1).

David was on the run again. Saul had been throwing his javelin indoors again—and in David's direction. Jonathan sent David into hiding while he checked on his father's mood, and the report wasn't good. This time, Saul had gone all the way over the edge in his bitter hatred toward David. He would not stop his vendetta until either he or David was dead.

It is at this point that David's life seems to come totally unraveled. First, David runs to Gath, the chief city of the Philistines, to seek the protection of the chief Philistine ruler, Achish. Achish was from Gath, and he had a good grasp of history. Who else was from Gath who figures significantly in David's life? The only hints I can give you are that he was extremely tall and he loved to behead people.

Yes, Goliath was from Gath. For some strange reason, David went right to Goliath's hometown—while carrying the very sword he had stripped from Goliath's body!

The Philistines were surprised for obvious reasons. In fact, King Achish himself came to the gates of the city to see if it was really the David "who had slain ten thousand." It suddenly dawned on David just how much danger he was in, and he became terrified. The only solution he could think of was to act like he'd gone mad! He began to salivate and drool all over himself while scratching on the walls and generally acting like a crazy man. And Achish looked at him and belly laughed, saying, "Look at that king of Israel! Forget about him—he's a rat in refuse." (See First Samuel 21:10-15.) The Philistines believed that one who kills a demonized person is vulnerable to possession by that same demon. Perhaps this explains David's wiley actions.

It was at that point that a dejected David slipped quietly into the cave Adullam. When the King James Version says David "escaped" to the cave Adullam, the word "escaped" means he "slipped" into it. He didn't really want to go there, but this was the best alternative he had. No one knows for sure precisely which of the countless caves riddling the massive limestone areas of south Israel is actually the "cave Adullam."

I've asked locals in Israel and consulted the work of many scholars, but there are just too many limestone caves in the wilderness of Engedi near the Dead Sea. You can put thousands upon thousands of sheep, goats, and people inside these caves. They seem to go on forever underground. So, we don't know precisely which one it was. I've searched through the area myself, hoping to discern which one of these caves is the "cave Adullam," but it was impossible to figure out.

It was the lowest moment of David's life. He must have thought, *Surely things can't get any worse!* But they did. When his family heard that he was hiding in the cave Adullam, they joined him. How would you like it if your own king (or president) had tried to kill you and you had to act like a madman to escape your country's greatest enemy? When you finally reached your new underground "home," you are hurting and licking your wounds. You're saying, "Dear God, I don't want to see or hear anybody! I'm taking the phone off the hook, Lord. I want to unplug everything. I don't want anything to do with anybody."

Then along comes Mom and Dad, plus 400 losers from all over the place! Worst of all, they're just like you—they're outcasts who are on the run from society for one reason or another:

> *And every one that was in distress, and every one that was in debt, and every one that was discontented, gathered themselves unto him; and he became a captain over them: and there were with him about four hundred men* (1 Samuel 22:2).

Would you have said, "Nobody home," or put out a sign that said, "Away for the duration"? Would you get an unlisted phone number and avoid public places? What did David do? The Bible says that David "became a captain over them." The man "after the heart of God" took them in as a shepherd takes in his sheep.

When we were laying the groundwork for the church we pastor now, we held prayer meetings in our home until we outgrew it. Then we moved to a small building in the area and held prayer meetings week after week for months. I'll never forget the day one of the ladies in the congregation said, "I believe I have a word from the Lord tonight." She read the passage in First Samuel 22 about the "four hundred" distressed and discontented who came to David. Then she said, "I believe that this is the quality and caliber of people God is going to bring into our church."

I thought, *Thanks a lot, lady. What are you talking about? Are you putting a curse on me?* Yet today, I thank God for every one of them.

David became a captain over them (see 1 Sam. 22:2b). The Hebrew word translated "captain" here is *sar*. It sounds just like the Russian word *czar*, but it doesn't refer to the supreme ruler of a nation. It refers to "a captain in the field"; somebody who got wet when his men got wet, who got muddy when his men got muddy. It describes a military leader who bivouacked in tents and lived in caves with his troops. David literally shared everything his 400 followers experienced.

When David "slipped" or fell into the cave Adullam, 400 other "losers" piled in there on top of him—and all of them were in debt or discontented. No one can ever accuse David of "starting a church to get the tithes." When the Bible says these men were "discontented" it is saying these men were "sour" on life. They were ready to give it all up. All this happened just as David began to experience the most hurtful moment of his life.

Adullam comes from the Hebrew root *dalah*. I love this word because it reminds me of Israel. Everywhere you go, you hear, "One dollah, please. One dollah." *Dalah* means "to dangle," like a bucket at the end of a rope. Have you ever been "at the end of your rope"? You may feel like you have been to Adullam several times already! Don't tell me you feel like you "live" there because Adullam is not for living; it is for learning.

Adullam was David's place of testing, growing, and learning. It was the hardest place in his life, and the only place that the Bible says he "fell" into. I think we all "fall" into tough testing times, but Adullam is just as necessary for reigning as Bethlehem.

If you tell me, "Dr. Cottle, I have my calling from God, and I have my anointing. Now I've made my beginning." That's wonderful. Do you know where you will get to go next? "Well, I'm going for the gold of my destiny! I've defeated my Goliath, you see. And I've found a friend that I can pour my life into and who will help me with my journey. I'm on my way to success."

Guess where you're going now—that's right: If you intend to reach Zion, then you're on your way to Adullam! You can always get sidetracked and entangled by money-making schemes, the accumulation of lands and houses, and the allure of success. But all of that will only rust or rot in your hands if you fail to fulfill your destiny and achieve the divine design dwelling within you. Frankly, anything that deters you from your divine destiny, you will live to curse. That quest is worth whatever it costs you. Like a mother who finally experiences the pleasure of holding her newborn baby in her arms, once you achieve your destiny you will forget all about the pain it took to get you to Zion.

"And [David] brought [his parents] before the king of Moab: and they dwelt with him all the while that David was in the hold" (1 Sam. 22:4). What happens in Adullam? The Bible says David was placed "in the hold" there. I like that. David was put "on hold" by the Holy Spirit. Yes, he had a "calling," and he had been "anointed" by the prophet Samuel. He had even killed his Goliath. It looked as if David was on his way to the top. If you're saying the same thing don't be surprised if God says, "That's right. Now slide over here on a back burner for a while. I have put all the ingredients for greatness in you—the meat is in there, the celery is in there, the potatoes are there. Everything that will make this pot roast is in there. Now, slide over on the back burner so you can just simmer for a while."

Without Adullam, you will never be worth anything. You will become an inedible, bland stew folks won't eat. Show me a person whose life has mellowed, and who has found a centerpoint; and I'll show you a person who knows suffering firsthand. Those who do not know suffering firsthand generally aren't worth listening to. It is a principle of life. Yet most of us spend our time groaning, complaining, and begging to get out of Adullam when it is the only place that we can learn certain lessons.

Adullam was both the worst and the best place of David's life. I've been to Adullam twice as far as I can tell, and I never want to go back! Yet I also thank God for taking me there. It was my fault. I deserved it. I needed it, but I don't ever want to need it again. I have to tell you that *qualities are developed in Adullam that cannot be developed anywhere else in life*! Don't beg God to get you out of

Adullam—ask Him to let you learn the lessons of Adullam so that when He brings you out in His good time, you will never need to go back.

David took Adullam seriously. That is why he took his mother and father to the king of Moab. That in itself is incredible! A Moabite was a Philistine, one of the most vicious enemies of Israel! Why did David think he could go to Mizpeh the king of Moab and leave his mother and father there while he was in the hold?

The Gospel of Matthew lists a genealogy or lineage of Jesus Christ that includes this passage: "And Salmon begat Booz of Rachab; and Booz begat Obed of Ruth; and Obed begat Jesse" (Mt. 1:5). Booz or Boaz was the father of Obed. David put his mother and his father in the home of his grandpa, Obed, who was a Moabite. He asked this king of Moab, "Let my father and my mother, I pray thee, come forth, and be with you, *till I know what God will do for me*" (1 Sam. 22:3b).

Adullam was and is a place of confusion. David was called and anointed, and he had handled Goliath. He was on the road to his destiny, but at that crucial moment in his life, he didn't have a clue about what God was doing in his life. David knew that he and God were going to get into a wrestling match of thunderous proportions in Adullam. He sensed that his life was going to be changed, shaped, and built for the rest of his future while he was there.

A lot of people in the Kingdom of God deny that there is an "Adullam" stage in the Christian life. The "faith message" came out a few years ago, and it is a good message that is right out of the Bible. However, some aberrations of the teaching claim that if something is "bad," that it isn't from God: "If it hurts, it's not God." I have to tell you that God sometimes leads us through Adullam because He has one objective for us: Zion. And the road to Zion runs through Adullam. That is just the way it is.

David got ready for Adullam by getting his priorities in order so he could focus on God and the lessons of Adullam. Do you realize that he had to stay there seven years? When he came out, however, he was a transformed person who commanded a crack army of 340,000 seasoned and well-disciplined soldiers! That's right, his original 400 men had grown to an army of 340,000 men! David was a king when he emerged from Adullam.

Earlier in this chapter, I said that David had been "placed on hold" by the Holy Spirit. This comes from the verse that refers to his stay in Adullam as "…all the while that David was *in the hold*" (1 Sam. 22:4). What does it mean to be placed on the "back burner" by the Holy Spirit? This is one of the greatest lessons I believe the Lord has ever taught me.

The Hebrew word translated as "hold" is *m-s-d*, sometimes appearing as *masad*, *matsad*, or *masodah*. (Hebrew is a "consonantal" language. The vowels were added only about a thousand years ago long after the biblical period, so we would know how to pronounce the words. There were no vowels in the original Hebrew text.)

Whenever you come into Adullam and are put on the "back burner" of God's stove, you need to understand that He is "growing" you. The Lord gave me a *rhema* of His Word in this passage. He said, "Adullam is the place for growing underground." When we started the church I now pastor, I walked one of the elderly ladies to her car after a prayer meeting and remarked that we had been praying for six or eight weeks. Then I said, "I think we've hit a plateau; we're not growing anymore." She looked at me and said, "Oh, Pastor, that's not true. We are growing now—more than ever." I thought to myself, *You can't count lady*, and I said, "The numbers are the same as they were four weeks ago. We need to keep growing." She just smiled and said, "*We're growing underground*, Pastor. We're shooting out roots into each others' lives. We're building the foundation in our relationships with each other so that when the fruit comes, we can bear it, and we can hold it." Adullam is a place for "growing underground."

We develop values in Adullam's darkness that can be pursued in the sunshine of a brighter day. When David was put "on hold" in Adullam, the outcome of that experience depended on David. One of the greatest truths the Lord ever showed me was this: When God put David on the "back burner," he could either make it a *masada* or a *masuda*.

Masada means "fortress." Specifically, it refers to the "briefing room" where generals come together to strategize for war. It is the heart and core of the warfare in a conflict. It is the "counsel chamber." This word also means "stronghold."

When you enter a time of testing, trouble, and trauma in your life, God is pushing you over on a "back burner" so He can build into you a fortress and a stronghold of His Word and of relationship with Him. That fortress and stronghold will become the very foundation of your life and ministry from that point forward! That is what happened with David.

However, David's stay in the "hold" could just as easily have become a *masuda* in his life. *Masuda* has the same letters, but is a different word. It means "a snare, a trap." If this passage was describing a failure in David's life, it would use the same "written word" we translate as *masada*, but the context and experience of David's life would establish its meaning as "a snare" instead of "a stronghold and fortress." What makes the difference? The meaning changes with the view or perspective that you take of the experience!

If you take the "Yah" view, if you look at your cave Adullam through God's eyes, you will see it as a powerful training ground and foundation for future ministry. If you take the "you" (or "me") view and pray, "God, I want to get out of here. Why did You put me here? Did You put me here to hurt me? I'm down and out, and nobody cares," then you will find yourself trapped in a *masuda*, a snare of failure. David was human. He actually said all those negative things at first, but he worked through it! It is not a sin to be human; it is a sin to refuse to go on up higher with God.

> *I cried unto the Lord with my voice; with my voice unto the Lord did I make my supplication. I poured out my complaint before Him; I shewed before Him my trouble* (Psalm 142:1-2).

David was transparent about his experiences in Adullam. When he said he "cried out" to the Lord, he used the Hebrew word, *za'aq*, which literally means "to shriek from anguish or fear." Have you ever done that? The Hebrew word for "showed" is *nasad*, which means "to make abundantly clear." David didn't want God to have any doubt about what he was talking about.

David was human, just like you and me today. He wrote Psalm 142 in the early days of his stay in the cave Adullam. Then, little by little, David began to get the "Yah" view of his life. He turned that experience into the greatest strength of his life and ministry! And from this experience, he learned to get God's view on every situation and circumstance. After this, he went to God for direction every time he fought a battle against the Philistines.

(By the way, the Philistines of today are the "principalities...powers...[and] rulers of the darkness of this world" spoken of in Ephesians 6:12. They are the Goliaths of our day—the demon spirits, our carnal nature, and man-made tradition.) David learned to search for God's understanding in every matter.

When God puts you "in the hold," He puts you there to test you and make you better. A test (*masada*) will make you better, but a temptation (*masuda*) will make you bitter. It's the same experience, but the way you take it will make the difference.

If you can learn how to deal with Adullam by getting God's view of what comes into your life, then you can turn it into your greatest victory. From this point on David took *masada* with him everywhere he went. Every time the Philistines came against David, the Bible said, "David went into the hold." He went into his *masada*. And every battle David ever fought from that time on was fought from *masada*. He fought with the knowledge of

God he learned at Adullam, the most important turning point of his life.

Like Joseph centuries before him, David could say to Saul and his pursuers, "But as for you, ye thought evil against me; but God meant it unto good [Gen. 50:20a]. The devil intended it to bring me harm, but God meant it for my good." In everything, particularly in Adullam, God is at work for the ultimate good of those who love Him and are "the called according to His purpose" (Rom. 8:28).

Your Adullam is designed to strengthen you (or weaken you if you keep your gaze on yourself). Your "cave" experience is designed for destiny (or destruction, depending on your heart attitude). The same experience can have two radically different outcomes depending on the viewpoint you take.

Everything that comes into your life has either a divine or a demonic handle on it. If you can find the right "handle" for your crisis, then God can use anything for your good. I have a little statement that might do you some good in your life: "You must be put on hold in order to get a hold of the divine destiny within you."

David's twenty-third Psalm, written while he was in the cave Adullam, holds a key to success in the midst of crisis. "The Lord is my shepherd…. I walk through the valley of the shadow of death…" (Ps. 23:1,4). Many people will tell you, "Well, the Lord is obviously not your shepherd, because He would never lead you through the valley of the shadow of death. No, He will only lead you to bliss and prosperity and plenty."

David said, "The Lord is my shepherd." The Hebrew word for "shepherd" is *rohe*. One of the names of God is *Jehovah-rohe*. This word means "one who takes me by the hand and leads me." The Good Shepherd walks with me. The Lord has me by the hand, and He is leading me as I walk through the valley of the shadow of death. A lot of people say, "Oh no, brother, not my God!"

Yes, your God loves you enough to take you through Adullam. I love Margaret F. Powers' story entitled "Footsteps"; it tells of a man who reached Heaven and began to look back over his life. He saw two sets of footprints until he came to a place where he had gone through a deep, dark valley, a gulch of horror and heartache. Puzzled, he said, "But Lord, look at that. There's only one set of footprints there. Lord, You were with me everywhere else, but You forsook me in that particular place." And the Lord said, "Look again, son. There's only one set of footprints because that's where I picked you up and carried you. Those are My footprints."

The Lord is your Shepherd, even when you walk through the valley of the shadow of death. God never said life would be a bed of roses, did He? If He did, He would warn you about the thorns. Isaiah the great prophet declared to Israel,

> *Who is among you that feareth the Lord, that obeyeth the voice of His servant, that walketh in darkness, and hath no light? let him trust in the name of the Lord, and stay upon his God* (Isaiah 50:10).

The word for "fear" in the Hebrew is *yare*, which means "to reverence."

You are reverent toward God, and you are a worshiper and an obedient servant of God, yet you sometimes walk in darkness and have no light. Darkness is confusion, or *sheol* in the Hebrew. The term *sheol* doesn't always mean "hell"; it actually refers to the essence of what hell is—confusion, purposeless, and meaninglessness. You walk in these things; you have no light. You are missing the important ingredients of purpose, focus, design, and desire. What do you do? God's Word says, "Let him trust in the name of the Lord, and stay upon his God" (Is. 50:10b).

The Hebrew word translated as "name" in this verse is *shem*. The cognate *shemen* is the word for the anointing oil that Samuel used to anoint David king of Israel, as we discussed earlier. The anointing of God grows out of the character of God. Thus the word *name* (or *shem*) means "God's character." It describes *who God is*, not *what He does*. Put your faith and your trust in the divine character of God when you're in that hard, troubled place called Adullam. He will never leave you nor forsake you. He'll be with you always.

Isaiah goes on to say, "And [let him] stay upon his God." That word "stay" is the Hebrew word *shaan*. It means "to lean on, to nail your life to, to fix and support yourself on God's character."

So where do you go when everything is confused, dark, and hurtful? Where do you turn when no one will acknowledge you or even admit that you are his friend? What do you do? You nail your life to the character of God.

W. Ian Thomas wrote a book entitled *The Mystery of Godliness*. In it he said, "When you're in (Adullam), a difficult place of your life, do not put your trust in God's will." He went on to explain, "Now, God's will is wonderful, but if you're in a time of confusion and you don't know what in the world is going on in your life, how can you be sure that you have a grasp of what God's will really is? So, you can't put your trust in God's will."[1]

"Don't even put your trust in God's work." We often say, "I know I'm a preacher, a prophet, and a teacher. I've got to get on with God's work. I'll just work my way through this thing." No, you need to understand what God is doing and saying to you. Get your mother, your father, and your children to a place of safety, and take care of the Adullam of your life. It's up to you to create room for God to work in your life!

A lot of people put on a "plaster of paris smile." They grin and bear it, and go straight to hell! Adullam becomes a *masuda* for them. Make room for God to work in your life if He has brought you to that place. Make room for Him and His purposes. "What will that mean?" You may discover you have to change jobs, or quit your present job. You might have to stop teaching the boy's class at church or heading up the youth group ministry. Let God do what He wants to do in your life. Do it.

If you are in the midst of Adullam, it is time for you to put your faith and confidence in His character, His person, in Him alone. He is the same "yesterday, today, and for ever" (Heb. 13:8). James 1:17 says that in Him there is "no variableness [nor] shadow of turning." You can trust

1. W. Ian Thomas, *The Mystery of Godliness* (Grand Rapids, MI: Zondervan Publishing, 1964), p. 9-22.

Him. In the Book of Malachi, God declares, "...I am the Lord, I change not" (Mal. 3:6a). Nail yourself into the divine character of God and stay there in His face.

We were praying for a woman's daughter one time, and this mother told me, "Dr. Cottle, I've done everything I know to do. I've done this, I've done that, and I've even done...! I've fulfilled everything that I know how to fulfill. What can I do now?" I told her, "Just stay at the heart of Jesus and let God do what He's going to do." (That takes a lot of faith.) Now that will turn a *masuda* into a *masada*. That will turn the worst place of your life into the best. It will transform your Adullam into a fortress for the rest of your life, a platform of victory from which you can fight the enemy and win.

What are the lessons to be learned in Adullam? It is ironic that David found the answer to his own needs by supplying the needs of others during one of the most stressful times of his life. This is an important principle in the Kingdom of God. If you try to hold on to your talents by "burying them" in the ground of your own personality and needs, then they will rot. On the other hand, if you take what you have, especially in times of pain, and sow into the lives of others who perhaps are not hurting as much as you, you will experience the miracle of God meeting your needs. He is glorified when you give away what you have to someone else. This law of "sowing and reaping" is a spiritual principle.

A friend of mine told audiences all around the world, "What do you need most in your life? Do you need compassion? Then take what little compassion you have—it may be just a thimble full—and give it to somebody else. In the process of pouring it out, like the widow's oil, it will grow and grow until you have more than you could ever use. Do you need mercy? Then take what little bit you have and sow it like a seed into some other needy person's life. Your mercy will grow in the sowing until you will have more than you could ever need for yourself and for others." This is a spiritual principle that David demonstrated right here in the cave Adullam.

David learned the lesson of compassion in Adullam. Without compassion, you will never be a leader in God's Kingdom. You will be too self-centered, and you will always be tempted to take everything in for yourself, whether the valued commodity is fame, respect, money, or leadership authority.

There are three kinds of people: takers, keepers, and givers. Which group winds up with more than they need in the end? Those who give away what they have. David learned to be a giver at the time of his greatest need.

When 400 losers, debtors, and discontented law breakers piled in on David, he forgot about his own needs. He saw their needs, and rolled up his sleeves to go to work. In the end, he made them into what Israel called "God's mighty men." They became the greatest fighting force that Israel ever had, and it was because David had learned compassion.

Second, David worked with those God brought him. David became a captain in the field over Israel's lowest outcasts. David could have said, "But I'm a king—I'm anointed. I'm not getting in that mud and dirt. I refuse to dig those trenches." A whole lot of anointed people will only work in the area of their anointing, believing anything else is "beneath them."

I had great hopes for a bright young man in our church who was full of promise and potential. He was like one of my own sons, and he eagerly did whatever I needed him to do. One time he slipped off somewhere and got into a meeting where some people told him he was a prophet. They said he should start focusing on his own work as a prophet.

Shortly after he returned from that meeting, a guest speaker was scheduled to come to our church. I normally like to pick up guest speakers at their hotel myself. Somehow I got tied up with some details, so I tossed my car keys across the desk and said to this young man, "Go and get the speaker. I'm too busy to break away." He said, "Oh, I can't do that." I looked up and said, "Say what?" Then he again told me, "I can't do that. I'm a prophet."

I recognized what was going on, so I said, "Okay, prophet, give me my car keys." Then I walked over to another young fellow who still works in the ministry today. I asked him, "Are you a prophet?" When he replied, "Not that I know of," I said, "Go get the speaker." The other young man kept his title but lost his servant's heart. What a tragedy!

Leadership does not reside in position;
Leadership resides in purpose and passion.

David realized that leadership resides in purpose and passion. He knew that purpose comes from revelation, and passion comes from relationship. I just gave you a whole university course in a few words. Did you get it? Leadership does *not* come from position! I know a lot of people who have leadership positions who are no more a leader than Mickey Mouse (in fact, when I think about it, they are a whole lot less qualified). True leadership comes from purpose and from passion.

Watchman Nee said, "The purpose of leadership comes through revelation." If God gives you the *rhema*, then you're the leader. Passion comes out of relationship with God in the Spirit. These are the ingredients of leadership.

David didn't need anyone to tell him he was king. He knew who he was, so he could roll up his sleeves and get right down into the muck and the grime to make things happen. His purpose was Zion. Now he was stuck in a cave in Adullam, and Zion seemed to be far away. He needed to learn the lessons of Adullam so God could bring him out. A lot of people live their lives stuck in a cave because they are unwilling to dirty their hands with anything except "*My anointing.*"

David accepted followers because they needed him, not because he needed them! These folks were in distress, in debt, and discontented, and he took them in. He wasn't looking for an easy road to victory. He didn't need a slave workforce to achieve "his vision"; and he wasn't searching for some shortcut to his destiny, or for some "sugar daddy" (wealthy sponsor) to pay his way. Now I have nothing against people giving generously to support God's work, so if you have a spare $600,000 or so, I know exactly where it can be put to good use. The principle is that we work with the people, materials, and resources that God brings.

Many ministers find it difficult to build their ministry on the basis of the gifts God provides—but that is God's way. Where there is no gift, there should be no ministry (because it isn't birthed of God). Don't look down the street at what "Brother and Sister Powerhouse" are doing, and say, "My, but they sure have a good, successful bus ministry. I think I will get into the bus ministry business too so I can build up my church."

If God wants you to get into the bus ministry, He'll plant a "gift" in the form of an anointed bus ministry pastor in your church and ministry. Whether you say anything or not, that fellow will begin to agitate for buses. Before long, you'll find yourself saying, "All right. All right. You may have one." Before you can turn around, he'll be back in your office saying, "I need another one, Pastor. We're growing too fast, and we have too many people for that one bus to handle." That's the way God-birthed ministry grows. If the gift isn't in the house, the ministry can't flow from the house. Any ministry in your church that has to be propped up and given mouth-to-mouth resuscitation every few months has problems. If it keeps pulling money out of other things, then give that flesh-driven work a decent burial. Put it out of its "ministry misery."

One of my favorite messages comes from Second Kings 4:1-7 and the story of Elisha and the widow's cruse of oil. One of Elisha's disciples in the school of the prophets had died, leaving his wife and two sons deeply in debt. Creditors were coming to take her two sons and put them into slavery to pay the debt. This widow called on the man of God for help, and Elisha the prophet responded. He looked around and asked her, "What do you have in the house?" She said, "I don't have anything in the house except a cruse of oil." A cruse of oil.

The Bible says we have this treasure in what? Earthen vessels (see 2 Cor. 4:7). Do you know what a "cruse" is? It's an earthen vessel. That is what you are too—an earthen vessel with the potential to be full of the oil of the Holy Spirit of God. That is what you have in your house. Every believer has this oil in his house. What do you have in the house? Elisha, the man of God, said, "Give it to me."

Now your first impulse might be to say, "This prophet deserves the left foot of fellowship—right out the front door. Who does he think he is to take for himself the last thing this woman owns?" A closer look reveals that there is a spiritual principle involved here. The fact is that you already have everything you need to meet every lack you will ever have! By the gift of God's grace, your Provision, the Risen Christ, is already inside you. He lives there in all of His abundance. By His Spirit, you are full of the oil of anointing. You are a cruse of oil.

"What can I do to meet my need?" Pour your oil into the needs of others. Pour it into every empty vessel you can find! Fill up every empty life that you can find in your community, your neighborhood, and the world. Pour out all of the oil you have! "Wait a minute, Brother Cottle. I'll run out!" No, you won't run out. In the very process of giving out of your need to meet the needs of others, your supply will grow until it is bottomless! The Bible says that widow had more than enough to pay her debts, with a supply left over for her and her sons to live abundantly from that day forward. It is an eternal principle of God.

David learned the principle and the miracle of compassion in the cave Adullam. He took in 400 lost and outcast men and poured himself into them. When he emerged from the wild and lonely caves of Engedi, he had transformed his ragtag band of losers into the greatest army Israel ever had! According to First Chronicles 12, David spent seven-and-one-half years with those men, and he converted his original band of 400 into a highly-trained army of 340,800 men by the time he left Adullam and went to Hebron to become king of Judah (talk about church growth)! This number doesn't even include all the wives and children.

Now if David did that in a cave in the wilderness, what can you do in the palatial church you belong to? David didn't have access to modern media tools, a college or seminary education, or publicity. He just had a "cruse of oil" that he poured liberally into people's lives. The more he poured, the more they came. The more they came, the greater they grew. When he finally came out of Adullam, he could have taken any kingdom in Israel that he wanted. His army was greater and even better trained than the standing army of Israel!

Let's improve our perspective before we move on past the lesson of compassion into the lesson of courage. David was called by God and anointed by the prophet Samuel when he was 17 years old. He was about 20 years old when he fought Goliath, according to the best evidence. He slipped into Adullam when he was 21 years old, and he left the cave of Adullam at the age of 28, after spending about seven and one-half years in the wilderness. He became king of Judah at the age of 30, and he was proclaimed king of Israel in his 37th year. David died and went to Heaven (the Bible says "slept with his fathers" [1 Kings 2:10]) at the age of 70. Every major episode and event in David's life happened at seven-year intervals.

The depth and quality of the relationships David shared with the men under his leadership are revealed in a remarkable passage in Second Samuel 23:13-17. It says that one day David was hot, tired, and thirsty while near the cave Adullam. He happened to remark (casually) to no one in particular, "Oh, if I only had a drink of water from Daddy's well in Bethlehem." (We all believe that the "best water" in the world is the water from home because we grew up drinking that water.)

Unknown to David, three of his "mighty men" heard him make that off-hand statement. The Bible says they got together and risked their lives to sneak right through the encampment of the Philistine army to bring David one canteen of Bethlehem water. The well was in the center of the enemy's camp! Those men loved their leader so much, and their lives were so intertwined with his destiny, that they thought nothing of risking their lives to please their leader and meet his need! This is the true Bible definition of a *sharath*, a "minister."

When these men offered David the water from his father's well in Bethlehem, he knew they had come within a hairsbreadth of losing their lives for his sake. He was a soldier. He knew that if any one of the men had made one sound, they would have all died a cruel death at the hands of their enemies. Most humbling of all, David knew they had risked their lives not to supply something he *needed*; no, they had knowingly risked their lives to supply something he had merely *wanted*!

David was so moved by their sacrificial gift that he took the water from them as they stood together in a circle—after he probably called everyone else to his side—and he poured it out on the ground as an offering to Jehovah God for their fellowship and relationship with each other. He symbolically offered back to God the loyalty and relationship God had given him with his men. It was all rooted in David's compassion for others. Compassion is a fundament of leadership.

Chapter 5

Courage and Character
Born of Compassion

True courage always grows out of compassion. There is an old story that circulated throughout the U.S. Marine Corps about a young Marine during World War II who was ducking the hail of bullets and shrapnel on the bloody beachhead at the Battle of Guadalcanal in the Solomon Islands. The U.S. Marines played a crucial role in this important battle that helped turn the tide of the war in the Pacific theater. This young Marine said, "My knees told me, 'I don't want to be here,' but I told them, 'I know, but you're going to be here anyway because we have to keep America free!' " This young Marine's compassion and purpose overrode his fear. The moral of the story is this: *You can't have courage without fear and compassion. Courage grows out of compassion.*

"Then they told David [in the cave of Adullam], saying, Behold, the Philistines fight against Keilah, and they rob the threshingfloors" (1 Sam. 23:1). These Philistines were just plain bad. They could have stolen the grain before the Israelites put it in the ground, but they didn't.

They could have stolen the corn after it was fully mature, and still on the stalk in the field. But they didn't do that. They waited for the poor Israelites to buy the grain, sow it, tend it, take care of it, break their backs plowing and hoeing it. They even waited for these farmers to harvest the grain and complete the threshing on the threshingfloor before grinding the grain. Then they would sweep down and take the harvest from their hands. These raiders were coldheartedly robbing the Israelite threshingfloors.

David immediately went to the Lord in prayer: "...Shall I go and smite these Philistines? And the Lord said unto David, Go, and smite the Philistines, and save Keilah" (1 Sam. 23:2). Now there was a problem. David's men said, "...Behold, we be afraid here in Judah: how much more then if we come to Keilah against the armies of the Philistines?" (1 Sam. 23:3) They were afraid they would get caught outside of Judah in Israel—with Saul and his army on one side and the Philistines on the other.

Then David inquired of the Lord yet again. And the Lord answered him and said, Arise, go down to Keilah; for I will deliver the Philistines into thine hand (1 Samuel 23:4).

This victory would have been much better if David could have gone into battle in simple faith, not knowing what the outcome would be. However, David yielded to the doubt and unbelief among these men who were not yet fully with their leader.

I thank God that David didn't take a committee vote. (You and I both know he would have lost that vote and

God's blessing too!) In a "democratic" church, David would have been voted out with a unanimous "no confidence" vote right then and there. What did David do? He went to the Lord in prayer again.

Yes, it is okay to ask questions of those in spiritual authority—as long as you obey. If you are disobedient, then you don't have the right to question. If you are obedient, then you have the right to question. These men questioned David's word from the Lord, but David still didn't ask them what to do. He just went back and asked the Lord again.

This time, the Lord said, "Arise, go down to Keilah; for I will deliver the Philistines into thine hand." They needed the answer before they would tackle the problem. Jesus would have told those men, "Oh ye of little faith!"

When David came back with God's answer this time, the whole army rose up in a mighty spurt of *divine courage*: "So David and his men went to Keilah, and fought with the Philistines, and brought away their cattle, and smote them with a great slaughter. So David saved the inhabitants of Keilah" (1 Sam. 23:5). When God spoke to David the second time that settled everything. There was no committee meeting, and no "majority vote" was taken. The Bible says they went with David, and that is to their credit. The lesson to be learned was David's lesson. David and his men had learned the lesson of courage.

After the victory, while David was in the city of Keilah, he got a word from the Lord. In First Samuel 23:9-10, the Bible says,

And David knew that Saul secretly practised mischief against him; and he said to Abiathar the priest, Bring

hither the ephod. Then said David, O Lord God of Israel, thy servant hath certainly heard that Saul seeketh to come to Keilah, to destroy the city for my sake.

Where did he hear this news? Whether David heard it by rumor or through a word from the Lord, he somehow sensed the danger of staying in a walled city with Saul and his army on the prowl. He knew that if Saul had his army encircle the walls of Keilah, then he would kill him for sure. He would never have escaped if Saul had trapped him in that small walled city.

David somehow knew that Saul was planning to do that very thing, so he called for Abiathar the priest and the ephod and asked the Lord, "Is Saul going to come down?" And God said, "Yes, he is." This is a "word of knowledge" in operation. Then David asked, "Lord, will the people of Keilah save their own necks by giving me over to Saul?" And God said, "Yes, they will" (see 1 Sam. 23:9-12).

Why did David go down there and risk his life for those ungrateful people? They were hardly worth saving! They definitely weren't worth David risking his life and the lives of his men—or risking the possibility of making widows out of the wives and orphans of the children they had left behind in Adullam. So why did they save those unworthy people?

The "lesson" was not for Keilah; it was for David. God wanted David and his men to learn the lesson of true courage. Courage comes when you act out of compassion and your action puts your own life on the line for someone else in a way that threatens your own security and safety. Very often, it may seem that your selfless sacrifice isn't really appreciated, but you go on regardless. David learned the lesson of courage in Adullam, and he emerged from the cave a different person from the one who had entered it over seven years earlier.

You may ask, "Didn't David already have a lot of courage? Didn't he face Goliath, and the lion and the bear?" Yes, he did. But at Keilah, David and his mighty men were fighting for someone else and not for themselves. David and his men weren't working for a reward this time. They were placed in jeopardy to learn God's lesson of true courage. This was probably one of the greatest lessons David ever learned.

The third lesson of Adullam concerned one of the most rare commodities in the modern world—godly character. Once again, God used the environment of wilderness caves and desperate circumstances to drive home this lesson in David's life. He did it by placing David's greatest and most dangerous enemy right in his hands under totally helpless circumstances—twice! In each situation, David faced a battle between the character of man and the character of God, for both seemed to be "right," but only one was the will of God.

The driving force behind Saul's relentless pursuit of David was Abner, Saul's general. He really hated David because when David killed Goliath and all the women started singing, "Saul has killed his thousands, but David has killed his ten thousands," Abner was the head of the army. Due to the public outcry, Saul demoted Abner and put David in his place as the head of the army. You can imagine how Abner felt about David. Abner was the same age of Eliab, David's older brother. He felt the same way about David that Eliab did.

It was in the middle of all of this heated rivalry, jealousy, and political jockeying, that God put Saul at David's absolute mercy twice.

The first test appears in First Samuel 24, when David was being hotly pursued by Saul and his army for the first time. David was hiding in a cave at Engedi with his men when Saul suddenly showed up with 3,000 soldiers! Saul walked right into the cave, just far enough inside the entrance to block the view of the army waiting outside. (He had no idea David and his men were hiding in cave passages on either side of him.)

*Then Saul took three thousand chosen men out of all Israel, and went to seek David and his men upon the rocks of the wild goats. And he came to the sheepcotes by the way, where was a cave; **and Saul went in to cover his feet**: and David and his men remained in the sides of the cave* (1 Samuel 24:2-3).

The Authorized Version isn't very clear in this passage, so most commentators traditionally say that Saul was taking a nap in the cave, which is rather ridiculous. The king didn't go inside that cave to take a nap while 3,000 men waited for him. Saul had to relieve himself. Further study of the Old Testament shows us quite clearly (and I'm not going to get into it) that Saul had a bowel problem (quite possibly IBS, Irritable Bowel Syndrome). He could not eliminate his body wastes without a great deal of effort and intensity. That is what he was doing inside that cave.

Saul was the king, and he was wearing his kingly garment during that military campaign. We know this because David cut off part of the hem from that garment later on. Obviously, there were no restrooms or portable toilets in the wilderness then (or today for that matter). While the 3,000 men under Saul's command simply stepped behind a tree or bush to relieve themselves, the king was expected to handle things differently.

The King James Version says Saul came into the cave to "cover his feet." This means he had to take off his royal cloak and lay it at his feet so he could focus on relieving himself in private.

Evidently, Saul was having a hard time. He was so focused on his problem that he didn't see or notice the 600 men who were hiding in that cave right next to him. The young men with David urged him to take advantage of the situation, but David refused to harm his enemy. Instead, he cut a big piece out of Saul's robe while his back was turned. The hem of the garment had the emblem of the king in it. When David did that, even though he said he wouldn't lift his hand against God's anointed, he did so in a very real sense because he took that emblem of the kingdom for himself.

This was more devastating than it seems at first reading. Do you remember Michal's reaction when she saw David dancing before the ark as it was brought into Zion? Israeli men in that day took off their outer garments before dancing, especially if they were costly royal or priestly garments. When David did this, he had his tunic and his underskirt left. Undoubtedly, what David did was pull up the flowing underskirt and tie it between his legs and crotch in the same way slaves did who worked in the fields or winepresses. It was considered to be an unsightly thing, and usually only slaves dressed that way. The most offensive part of this action was that it exposed the upper portion of a man's legs. This portion of a free man's anatomy, especially that of a public or religious leader, was only to be seen by wives and concubines in the privacy of the home.

Michal was legally right but spiritually wrong to despise David. She knew etiquette and protocol. She was absolutely, pristinely perfect, but she was also spiritually barren. When David cut Saul's robe, he set up an embarrassing situation for the king. When Saul put that robe back on and walked out of the cave in front of his soldiers those men saw something they had never seen before; they saw the upper legs of the king. This, in effect, put King Saul on a slave's level. They saw what only slaves bared to the public, and it commonized the king.

So David did touch God's anointed. He didn't touch Saul's person, but he touched his office. He didn't try to kill the man, but he did damage his office. It was at this point that David's heart "smote" him. He felt guilt for what he had done. When Saul left the cave, David called to him, "Abbi, abbi." You can read it in the Hebrew. "My father, my father." Then he held up the piece of the king's garment in his hands, and Saul must have turned around immediately. David told him, "I could have killed you. I could have taken your life, but I refused to stretch forth my hand against God's anointed," as he held up the evidence. Saul was obtuse, of course. He wasn't open to the truth, nor did he understand the depth of David's mercy. He began to weep as he finally admitted, "You're more righteous than I. Forgive me, David. I won't try to kill you again. You can go your way. You're a free man." Then he turned his army around and went away. Of course, it was all a lie, but David had passed the first test.

Since Saul had not changed in his heart, only two chapters later we see that the king once again dispatched his elite force of 3,000 soldiers to scour the wilderness for David. The weary David said he felt like he was being hunted down like a flea or a partridge (see 1 Sam. 26:20b). Once again, he was about to face a test of character as Saul again walked right into his hands.

So David and Abishai came to the people by night: and, behold, Saul lay sleeping within the trench, and his spear stuck in the ground at his bolster: but Abner and the people lay round about him. Then said Abishai to David, God hath delivered thine enemy into thine hand this day: now therefore let me smite him, I pray thee, with the spear even to the earth at once, and I will not smite him the second time. And David said to Abishai, Destroy him not: for who can stretch forth his hand against the Lord's anointed, and be guiltless? ... The Lord forbid that I should stretch forth mine hand against the Lord's anointed.... So David took the spear and the cruse of water from Saul's bolster; and they gat them away, and no man saw it, nor knew it, neither awaked: for they were all asleep; because a deep sleep from the Lord was fallen upon them (1 Samuel 26:7-9,11-12).

Joab's youngest brother, Abishai, volunteered to sneak into Saul's camp with David. This young stallion was just like Joab and the rest of his brothers—he was a murderous thug. He was a good soldier under the guidance of strong and moral leadership, but he was an ungodly counselor and leader on his own. He wanted David to strike down the king and thank God for the opportunity, or at the very least, allow him to do the deed. His older brother, Joab, had been a childhood buddy of both Saul and Abner, the king's military commander. All three were older than David. Joab and Abner grew up hating each other, and they were always competing with each other.

This younger brother of Joab said, "Look at this, David. This is fantastic! God has done it again. Saul is at your mercy! God is handing you your destiny on a silver platter!"

Warning: "Destiny" is *never* served on a silver platter! There is no shortcut to destiny.

Abishai said, "Look at this. Let me end your troubles with one thrust of my spear! You are only one swift blow away from the throne of Israel and the end of all this running!" David said, "I can't do that. I won't lift my hand against God's anointed."

This time, David (only) took the king's javelin and canteen. He didn't damage Saul, but he damaged Abner's reputation by taking Saul's provisions for war while the king's chief protector slept at his side. Again, David called to Abner from a safe distance, throwing cutting words at the military leader who hated David with a vindictive vendetta. David was saying, "If I were King Saul's general, no one would ever come this close to taking his life." What a humiliating thing this was for Abner. Then he said, "Abbi, abbi, father, father, again the Lord delivered you into my hand, but I would not take your life nor lift my hand against God's anointed" (see 1 Sam. 26:4-14).

David could have short-circuited the test of Adullam and come out before his time by simply acting contrary to God's character. The first time David spared Saul's life he felt guilty after cutting off a part of Saul's robe. The Bible says David's heart "smote" him. Any time you take your destiny into your own hands, you are taking God's will past God's character. Any time you take God's will or work past God's character, you will have problems. You can never get to a good destiny through bad means. David learned this lesson in Adullam.

The central principle is simply this: God never leads us to do anything that is contrary to His character. Abishai the brother of Joab told David, "Look at what God has done. He has put the kingdom into your hands, not once, but twice. All you have to do is just take it. Just do this one thing—let me kill your enemy. Let me remove the obstacle to your destiny."

How many times would you like to do that? "If I could just get that guy into the right position and push him over the edge!" No, God will never lead you to do anything that is contrary to His character. The ends do *not* justify the means. In God's Kingdom, both ends and means must be in line with divine character.

God's will never operates outside God's character. The character of God must be the glass through which we view everything we do. If we can't see it cleanly through the divine nature of God, we better not do it.

The conclusion of Adullam was nearly as dramatic as the lessons learned there. After Saul left with his army, the hunted and hounded David said, "...I shall now perish one day by the hand of Saul: there is nothing better for me than that I should speedily escape into the land of the Philistines..." (1 Sam. 27:1). It is easy to understand his doscouragement. Had Saul's army kept after David for one more day, they might have caught and killed him. Saul had to rush his army to the far side of Israel to meet Philistine invaders, giving David a chance to move his entire band into Philistine territory.

It seems clear that the Lord used the Philistines both to save David's life and to fulfill the prophesied end of Saul's reign over Israel. David went free and Saul went out with his sons to wage a massive campaign against the Philistines. Saul went to battle in a Philistine chariot driven by horses, although God had forbidden Israel to put their trust in chariots and horses (see Is. 31:1). Saul fought like a Philistine general! He used the methodology of the enemy to fight the war of God.

While David learned his lessons in Adullam, Saul drove himself further and further away from the presence of God. The end finally came when Saul became so afraid at the sight of the Philistine army, that he consulted with the witch of Endor. Then he met the Philistines in battle on Mount Gilboa—apart from God's guidance and protection.

The Bible tells us the Philistine archers were able to find their mark and wound King Saul despite the Philistine armor he was wearing. When all hope was lost, and all of his sons had been cut down, Saul begged his armor bearer to strike him down before the Philistines could do so, but the armor bearer was afraid to kill his own king. In the end, Saul fell on his own sword and brought about his own destruction, just as he had done in his walk with God (see 1 Sam. 31:3-6). The only survivors from his household were his son, Ishbosheth (the "man of shame"), and Jonathan's son, Mephibosheth.

As the Philistines began to advance on the royal palace, the maid charged with carrying Jonathan's son to safety panicked. As she ran in fear, carrying little Mephibosheth in her arms, she accidentally dropped him. His injuries were so severe that he was lame in both feet for the rest of his life. She fled to a place called *Lodebar*, which means "nowhere." Mephibosheth remained there in the care of a "foster" family in the middle of "Nowhere" until David came to the throne a few years later. King David began to search for any survivors from the house of Saul for the sake of Jonathan. He brought this "nothing from nowhere" who was lame in both his feet and set him at the king's table for the rest of his life.

David learned character in Adullam by learning the three great lessons of the cave "at the end of his rope." He learned compassion, courage, and character. These godly traits are just as important as calling, anointing, and beginning. If you're going to get to Zion (and I believe in my heart that you want to), then you will have to go through

Adullam! The lessons of Adullam, tough though they may be, are vital to the fulfillment of your destiny: Learn everything God wants you to learn about compassion, courage, and character. David learned these lessons, and God Himself called this very human leader "a man after Mine own heart." He didn't say this about any other man—until now. Today, God is working to raise up an entire generation of men and women who are "after His own heart," and He wants you and me to be in that number.

Part III

Hebron (The Place of Alliances)

The Place of Commitment, Relationships, and Covenant

Chapter 6

Judah: The Covenant With Failure

At the time of this writing, the city of Hebron is in Palestinian hands. Yet in David's day, this ancient city on a hill marked the second great phase of David's life and his advance toward Zion and the throne of Israel. After David had learned the three lessons of Adullam—compassion, courage, and character—he did something that had already become a hallmark of his life.

> *And it came to pass after this, that David inquired of the Lord, saying, Shall I go up into any of the cities of Judah? And the Lord said unto him, Go up. And David said, Whither shall I go up? And He said, Unto Hebron* (2 Samuel 2:1).

David never took a major step without first "inquiring of the Lord." Isn't that interesting? David had a word from the Lord, a *rhema* from God, for every major enterprise in his life. Perhaps that is why we still remember him today even though hundreds of other great leaders have been long forgotten.

The Hebrew word *amar* shows up virtually every time you read about David in the Old Testament. That is because this word means "says" or "saith." Any time you see phrases like "And David said..." or "And God said..." you are almost certain to find *amar* in the original Hebrew text. It is the Hebrew version of the Greek word *rhema*. David never went anywhere or did anything without a *rhema* from the Lord (except for the times he sinned or disobeyed God, as in his sin with Bathsheba and his decision to conduct a census of Israel contrary to God's instruction).

> *So David went up thither, and his two wives also, Ahinoam the Jezreelitess, and Abigail Nabal's wife the Carmelite. And his men that were with him did David bring up, every man with his household: and they dwelt in the cities of Hebron. And the men of Judah came, and there they anointed David king over the house of Judah* (2 Samuel 2:2-4a).

David's new assignment from the Lord was to go up to "Hebron." David immediately obeyed, and he took his family, and his men and their families with him. Isn't that wonderful? These people had become so intertwined with David's life that they went wherever he went.

Hebron means "alliance." It is the place of commitment, relationship, and covenant. If you look at a topographical map of Israel, you will find something that is fascinating to me. Hebron is one of the highest, most inaccessible places in all Palestine. It is higher topographically than Zion or Jerusalem. No one ever "slipped or fell" into Hebron like David "slipped" into Adullam. In fact, the only way you can get into Hebron is to desire to go there and work hard to get there! It is true today, and it was especially true in the days when you either walked or rode a camel or horse.

Adullam is a place of testing, trouble, and trial. You can slide or fall into that low spot any time. Hebron is different. You cannot "fall" into a high place. Hebron has to be earned. Hebron is difficult to achieve but necessary to reign.

Hebron is the Hebrew word for "alliance." You don't fall into commitment. You don't fall into alliances or covenant. You have to create and forge covenant. While your experiences in Bethlehem and Adullam help forge the vertical relationship between you and God, it is Hebron that will forge the horizontal relationships you share with others.

It isn't enough just to be ready spiritually. It isn't enough just to be ready with God to do warfare in this world. You have to build relationships, covenants, and commitments with other people to be "in balance." You can't be full of animosity, venom, hatred, and misunderstanding toward other people and expect to succeed in ministry and in the Kingdom of God.

Hebron marks the place where you forge alliances to help you "keep" the progress you've made in your relationship with God. This vitally important area always follows the vertical. Your relationships with people come after you develop a right relationship with God. This qualifies and equips you to take care of your relationships with other people.

Two important things happened when David went up to Hebron, and they set the stage for the three lessons he learned there. First, David became Judah's king at Hebron. And second, he learned that somebody else got the "big prize" of the throne of Israel—his destiny.

"And the men of Judah came, and there they anointed David king over the house of Judah" (2 Sam. 2:4a). David is called the lion of the tribe of Judah. When the elders of the house of Judah made David king, they were proclaiming him king of his own tribe and house, not king over the *nation* of Judah. At that time, Judah had been so battered and beaten down by Israel, the Philistines, and everybody else who came along, that this tribe didn't even have an army! They were weak, poor, and insignificant. Frankly, it wasn't much of an honor to be "king" of Judah at that point.

When the elders came to make David king of Judah, it wasn't any big deal. Put yourself in David's sandals for a moment. There you are, you're called and anointed to be king over all of Israel. You've defeated and killed a Goliath in man-to-man combat, you've won international acclaim as a warrior and master general of the king's army, and now you have your own army that is larger than the king's! You've just finished a seven-and-one-half-year period of living on the run, scrambling for your life while caring for thousands of other people. Along the way you've paid the price to learn the lessons of courage, compassion, and character.

Obviously, you're ready for "First Church, Central Cathedral, Times Square." You've already lived in a king's palace, worn a general's stars on your lapel, and your hide bears the scars of survival in impossible situations. Now some guys come up and basically name you the Master Teacher for the junior boy's class in the trailer at the end of the parking lot! That is what happened to David.

If this hasn't ever happened to you, then I have some good news and some bad news for you. I'll give you the bad news first: If this kind of disappointment has not come to you yet and you're headed for Zion, it will certainly happen somewhere along the way. But now for the good news: Judah isn't for living; it's for learning. The truth is that David's coronation in little Judah actually represented failure, not success! Judah represents the "small" assignment, the "insignificant place," the "small beginning," the "second-best position" that most people despise and avoid at all costs. Obviously, God doesn't think like man thinks. In His plan, no one is fit to reign in Zion until they are faithful in Hebron.

The second important thing that happened while David and his troops were in Hebron was that someone else got the "big prize." David's archenemy, Abner, the general of Saul's army, had made himself strong for Saul. He was the man who had driven Saul's troops day and night, hunting down David like a dog nipping at a flea on his back. He hated David with an undying hatred.

After Saul fell in battle, Abner was in charge. As general of the army of Israel, he became the most powerful man in Israel (or so he thought). He only had one problem—the people wouldn't let him rule because he was not royalty.

When Abner heard that David had been made king of Judah, Abner knew he had better do something quickly or the people of Israel would begin to say, "Well David, you are already the king of Judah—why don't you just become king over the whole shooting match?" So Abner quickly grabbed the only son Saul had left—his "good for nothing" son, *Eshba'al*, or *Ishbosheth*.

Esh, or *Ish*, means "a (little) man, as opposed to Adam, a significant man." He called himself Eshba'al, the "man of Baal." Eshba'al undoubtedly took this name out of spite for his father. The word *ba'al* was the Philistine term for god. So this outcast son of Saul walked around calling himself "the man of Philistia's god." He was saying, "My father is the king of Jehovah's people, but I want you to know I'm Baal's man."

This is the portrait of a turncoat. His name was so offensive to his father and the Jewish people that they refused to call him by his name. They wouldn't call him Eshba'al because they didn't acknowledge Baal, so they created another name for him, *Ishbosheth*. It was a play on words of course. The Hebrew word *bosheth* means "shame." When it is combined with *Ish*, which like *Esh*, also means "little man," you have *Ishbosheth*, the "little man of shame."

Abner chose a man who had shamed his father, his family, and his nation. He tried to make him the new king of Israel in name only—and what a name it was. Abner only grabbed him because he had Saul's blood in his veins, and it was the only way he could stay the rising tide of divine destiny in the life of David. He never believed or said Eshba'al was actually worthy to rule.

People will do a lot of things to keep you down too, when they see the rising tide of destiny in your life. But the truth is, nobody and nothing can stop God's divine destiny from rising up in your life except you!

While Judah was considered an insignificant, poor, and weak nation, Israel was important, rich, and strong. Abner wanted to keep David out of the throne of Israel at any cost—even if it meant putting this wimpy "champion of Baal" on Israel's throne. Eshba'al had never fought in the army with his father like Jonathan or his other two brothers. That is why when these great warriors all died together with their father in a battle against the Philistines, nobody ever mentioned Ishbosheth. He wasn't anywhere close to the battlefield.

Abner went against the wishes of God and everyone in Israel to plant a cowardly, devil-worshiping outcast on Israel's throne in a desperate attempt to thwart David's destiny. In the face of this adversity, David learned to cut a covenant with failure in Judah. He learned how to use failure for the advancement of destiny. Failure is going to come. And every great leader or servant of God must learn how to deal with failure. You can't let failure stop you. A very good friend taught me this lesson, with a good dose of humor to "help the medicine go down." Charles Greenaway is in Heaven now (probably laughing at everything I do). He was one of the greatest missionaries to Africa of all time. Charlie used to say, "Listen, man, when you blow it big and they've tarred and feathered you, and are running you out of town...just get to the front of the crowd and pretend you're leading the parade!"

Learn how to "fall forward" in failure: Don't let failure stop you. I heard a man demonstrate failure by walking across a platform. He said, "Now folks, I'm failing. This is failure. The only way I can walk is to get myself off balance and fall forward. That's failure. If I didn't catch myself, I'd fall down. Every step is falling, yet I can't move forward unless I fall. Every step represents a fall and the process of catching myself in some failure. That is the only way we make progress in life."

Walking is "falling forward" in failure. Don't fall backwards; fall forward in failure. David failed in every way you can imagine. Abraham failed miserably. Moses failed miserably. Every great man and woman of God has failed miserably, and yet they were able to get on top of their failures instead of allowing their failures to get on top of them. They were able to use failure as a springboard to their destiny. Everyone who reads these words has failed—including the author.

No one fails "for the fun of it" because failure is not fun, but the lessons of failure are necessary. We will all fail, but when we do, we must get on top of it. There are three steps to harnessing the lessons of failure. First, remember that the blood of Jesus Christ "cleanse[s] us from all unrighteousness" (1 Jn. 1:9). Second, remember that Jesus sanctifies and cleanses you "with the washing of water by the word" (Eph. 5:26). Third, you must continue in fellowship and "walk in the light, as He is in the light" (1 Jn. 1:7). David learned how to deal with failure, and he dealt with it positively. It is also part of our training for reigning.

Judah represented failure for David. It was a "second best" assignment, a substitute for what he knew was his ultimate divine destiny. Yet God used this supposed "detour" as a vital training ground for the man who would become Israel's greatest king. When David cut a covenant with his own lowly tribe, he had a highly trained army of 340,800 warriors, while Judah had no army at all. The tribe of Judah was getting a "good deal," because David's army became their protection from hostile acts by Israel and the Philistines—at little cost to them. Judah had everything to gain, while David stood to gain virtually nothing.

Most people in the world are getters and takers, or even stealers. There just aren't many "givers" out there. It is clear that God will only work through givers, and David was a giver. That is why God Himself—not David, Israel, or the other writers of the Psalms and the Book of Kings—declared in person, "I have found David the son of Jesse, a man after Mine own heart, which shall fulfil all My will" (Acts 13:22).

David proudly accepted Judah and became Judah's king. He behaved in Judah as if he were already reigning in Zion. He took that "junior boy's class" and made it the best junior boy's class in the city! Proudly accept the small place, and realize that man didn't put you there. God put you there because He has a lesson for you to learn. Once you learn that lesson, nothing any small-minded person can ever do to you will stop the rising tide of divine destiny in you.

Embrace the small place and make the most of it. Learn its lessons, and learn how to fall forward in failure. If you're going to Zion, you will go through Judah, and

Judah is a place of failure. Failure is inevitable, but if you can just learn to take that failure and use it as a stepping stone to your ultimate destiny, then that failure will serve you like success never could. David behaved in Judah as though he were already in Zion.

Suppose you have a tiny group of people on "the back side of nowhere" who have accepted you as their spiritual leader and authority. Like many others, you could say, "Well, I'm the best thing that ever happened to these folks. They never heard anybody preach and teach like me. So, whatever I do and say will be fantastic to them. I think I'll just play golf, go fishing, and take it easy. I'll just give them whatever comes because that's the best they've ever had anyway."

This kind of attitude in a minister or shepherd hurts the flock of God because he doesn't give them what they need. But in the end, the person he will hurt the most is himself. Why? *He will be in Zion what he has become in Judah.* Do you take shortcuts and only perform at your best when everyone is watching? Do you refuse to study and pray for Wednesday night prayer meeting, and instead you "choose to save it" for the Sunday morning service? You say you don't need to fast and pray. Do you just put on a performance? Beware: You are creating the character that must sit on the throne of destiny in Zion. You'll never be any better in Zion than you become in Judah!

I've known people who have cut moral corners in the small place, and justified their actions by saying, "Look, I'm not going to be here long, and I'll never run into these people again." They mistreated and walked on the people. I couldn't help but think of my grandma's wise words of warning, "Watch out who you walk on when you climb the ladder of life, because you will probably meet them when you're coming down and they're going up."

David behaved in Judah spiritually, morally, and ethically as though he were already in Zion. He gave the same exquisite care to Judah that he later gave to Israel. (Jeremiah 29:4-14 is a magnificent passage of Scripture that contains wonderful principles of behavior for those times when you find yourself in a "hard place".) God never promised us that life would be a bed of roses, but He did promise He would be with us. Use every hard place and failure as a stepping stone to your ultimate destiny.

Joshua, the leader who led Israel across the Jordan into the promised land after the death of Moses, belonged to the tribe of Joseph. When the 12 tribes went into Israel, the land was parceled out equally as Moses had told them to do, but the tribe of Joseph was almost as big as all the other tribes combined at that point.

The tribal elders came to Joshua and they said, "Joshua, you're a part of us. We want you to give us more of the land because we're bigger than all the rest of them." Joshua's answer in Joshua chapter 17 gave several key principles for "advancement in the Kingdom." Basically, Joshua told them, "Brothers, you still have giants in your land. You haven't even cleaned out the giants from the land you have now. Once you have cleaned out all the giants in your own land, then come back and talk to me about extending the borders of your tents." This sounds like a spiritual law, doesn't it?

Have you ever said, "If I were the pastor, I would do thus and so"? No, you would do exactly what you're doing now! Where you are, who you are, and what you are now will determine where, who, and what you will be tomorrow. Today, in your Judah, you are building the character and lifestyle that you will take with you to reign in Zion. There are two other covenants or alliances in Hebron that are closely associated with the covenant with failure. David agreed to accept the throne of the house of Judah, but he still faced the challenges of a covenant with his greatest living enemy, Abner; and with a force that has destroyed many of the famous men and women in human history: the force of personal fame and success.

Chapter 7

Abner and Israel: Covenants of Forgiveness and Fame

Life in Hebron, "the place of alliance," is primarily concerned with making commitments, entering relationships, and cutting covenants. David had already cut a "covenant of failure" with Judah when he accepted the throne of a poor, weak, and disorganized tribe. Yet he was about to cut an even more astounding covenant with his most deadly enemy.

Before you can ever reign effectively in Zion, you have to work out your "horizontal relationships" (relationships with other people). Someone said that George Washington claimed he had never won a single battle. He simply "put together a series of defeats" to win the war! You may lose battle after battle in your journey to Zion, but just make certain you do not lose the war. *The key is to learn how to "fall forward" in failure.*

David faced a major challenge when Abner, the general who had personally chased him through the hills and caves of Engedi for seven and one-half years, asked him to become an ally under a covenant of peace (see 2 Sam. 3:12). After Saul's death and Abner's sudden appointment of Ishbosheth as king over Israel, the Bible says Abner "made himself strong" for Saul's house and conducted continuous war against David's army in Judah.

Everything changed when Abner's puppet king, Ishbosheth, accused Abner of having sexual relations with the late King Saul's concubine, Rizpah. Abner was so outraged, even though the charge was true, that he told Ishbosheth he was immediately transferring his loyalty to David, and that he would do everything he could to put David on the throne of Israel. "And Abner sent messengers to David on his behalf, saying, Whose is the land? saying also, Make thy league with me, and, behold, my hand shall be with thee, to bring about all Israel unto thee" (2 Sam. 3:12).

The second lesson David learned in Hebron was how to deal with forgiveness. This is a lesson we all must learn. There was a time in my life when I believed that certain people were out to ruin me. One of them in particular seemed determined to hurt me. The plan was set in motion while I was in Israel on a study assignment.

On my return, my associate from the office who came to pick me up at the bus station (the ice and snow were so bad that the airlines were grounded) told me he couldn't take me to my office. So I asked, "Hey, who is in charge, you or me? Take me to my office, please." Then he said, "I can't do that. Your boss said I was to take you home. You're fired!"

Sure enough, I was fired. I learned that I had suddenly become dispensable, and was no longer needed in my high position. It seemed my former boss was determined to go a couple steps further—he wanted to discredit me as well.

I will never forget the next two or three months. I felt incredibly alone. It is amazing how fast your friends can flee from you when you're down. It got so bad that I used to dial my own telephone number just to see if it would still ring! I was praying one day underneath the desk in the basement of my house when God spoke to my heart. (It is amazing how comfortable it feels to crawl under your desk and lie down on the basement carpet when you're really down.) I hate to admit that I felt that low, but that is the way it was.

As I prayed there under my desk, my hand was lying on the carpet with the palm up. Then the Lord said, "Look at your hand, son." When I looked at my open hand, He said, "There are five men walking in your hand right now because they've lifted their hands against My anointed." Please understand that these men were God's anointed too. You are God's anointed, and if I wrong you, then I'm in the palm of your hand. To say someone is "in the palm of your hand" represents or stands for authority. When you wrong someone, you come under that person's spiritual authority. If he wishes, that person can crush you, because you have wronged him, although God would prefer to teach that individual something more of the cross through relinquishing the right of retribution.

God said, "Now, son, they're walking in your hand. They are vulnerable to you because they have genuinely hurt you." Then He said, "Now, what are you going to do?" Then the Lord said, "Son, I want to remind you of one thing. Whatever you do to them will be done to you. If men don't do it, angels will. If angels don't do it, then I will. As for these men, they are going to reap what they have sown to you." When God asked me, "What are you going to do, son?" I thought of David, who often prayed for the death of his enemies and for vengeance, but then I was reminded that he and I live on two opposite sides of the cross.

Paul said that we don't wrestle against flesh and blood (see Eph. 6:12). God was saying to me, "Now, you can either crush them or you can breathe life into them. But whatever you do to them is what will be done to you." I chose to breathe life into my enemies, and I'm grateful that I did. Just a few days later, the phone rang, and I heard the familiar voice of an old friend of mine on the other end. Harvey weighed about 270 pounds, and he sometimes wore bib overalls and drove a pickup truck. He was a genius with an impressive I.Q., and he was a business man *par excellence*.

When I met him, he didn't have two nickels to rub together, but I watched him become a millionaire almost overnight. He became a part of the church I was pastoring, and he became my friend. I happened to mention to Harvey that as I drove to work along a particular street, I would always see a big open field with some ugly shacks on it and think, *Man, that's an eyesore. Somebody ought to do something*. That was all I said.

Harvey drove by that field once or twice, but when he looked at that field he saw something totally different. He saw a Walmart shopping center there! I watched as my friend Harvey went to each person who owned a little shack in that field. He'd say, "How much is your house worth?" If they said, "Well, my house must be worth $20,000 or $25,000," then Harvey would reply, "Okay, I'll give you $40,000." I watched these folks look around as if to say, "Mama, come quick. We've got us a fish now!" Then Harvey would say, "Here, here is $25 cash. I want a six-month exclusive option on this land." That man spent a grand total of $150 and managed to tie up 13 acres of prime property in one afternoon!

After that, Harvey sat down in front of his trusty computer with his son, who was as brilliant as he was. Then those two literally created a computer design for a Walmart shopping center. I'll never forget the night my doorbell rang and someone started banging on my front door at midnight. *What in the world?* I thought as I grabbed my ball bat and headed for the door. Sleepily, I muttered, "Who are you and what do you want?" as I opened the door.

There stood my friend with his completed and packaged Walmart plans in his arms. "Pastor," he said, "would you lay your hands on this and pray? I've got an appointment tomorrow morning with Sam Walton in North Carolina. I'm going to present this proposal to him."

I said, "Jesus, bless it. And Father, bless it. In Jesus' name. Amen." Then I said, "Good night, Harvey. Good night." Harvey took off for his meeting, and I didn't see him for several days. When Harvey came back, he had $1.3 million in his pocket. His family immediately moved to Phoenix.

Once again, Harvey was calling me on the phone from Phoenix. "Pastor, there's an airplane ticket with your name on it out at the airport. I got a problem down here that I need your help and advice on." Before I could crawl out from under my desk to turn him down, he said, "Pastor, please, don't disappoint me!"

Now Harvey knew what had been happening. Somehow he had found out about everything, and he knew perfectly well that I didn't have a thing to do and nowhere else to go. No one else was even calling me. So that wily brother said, "I've got to have you. You're the only one who can help me. Now, Pastor, look, I need to run. You get the airplane ticket," he said. "I'm going to be at the airport waiting for you about four o'clock this afternoon." Click. Harvey just didn't leave me any option.

I called my faithful wife on the phone. She was working, teaching school, to pay our bills while I struggled to get my life back together and get back into the ministry. She just said, "I think you should go." She didn't ask any questions. She simply said, "You should go. You need him now."

So I got on the airplane and flew to Phoenix. Sure enough, when I got there a great big man beside a great big Cadillac stood there with a great big smile on his face. Harvey kind of enveloped me in a 270-pound bearhug and squeezed me real good. I hadn't had a hug like that in a long time, and it made me feel tremendous considering the circumstances I was in.

Then Harvey told me to hop in his car, and he started driving me around Phoenix. He said, "Pastor, the Lord has helped us get this and do that..." as he led me on a grand tour through his spacious offices. He even took me out on a mountain and said, "Our church has purchased this. The Lord let me help to get the down payment for it. This is where we're going to build a 7,000-seat church auditorium."

Then we got back in the car and drove around some more. It was a Wednesday, and I wasn't even thinking about mid-week prayer meeting, but Harvey wheeled that Cadillac right into his church parking lot and stopped. Then he said, "Come on, Pastor, we're going in." I said, "Oh no, I'm not going in there. I'm not ready for this, and I'm definitely not ready for that pastor of yours [Tommy Barnett]. He's always smiling, and full of life and energy. He's always bouncing, and it's sickening. I know him, and he knows me. And I don't want to go in there."

"Now, come on, Pastor," Harvey said, "we'll only stay a little while." Then two big hands kind of "pulled" me out of the car. (Well, what could I do about it?) We went in and he sat down first. When Harvey sat down, his two massive arms went out to the side, so I got behind one of those arms. *Nobody will ever see me here*, I thought, *because I can hide behind him.*

I was trying to hide behind Harvey's arm as the service got started when Pastor Tommy Barnett came in with his eternal or ever-present smile. He looked around and immediately spotted me. "Dr. Cottle, is that you?" he asked as I tried to hide a little better. "Brother Ron Cottle, is that you? Come up here, Brother Ron!" I reluctantly walked up there as everyone applauded. (I had preached in that church before.) Then Pastor Barnett said, "Brother

Ron, what has God been doing in your life?" I said, "Well, you wouldn't believe it. You just wouldn't believe." Not to be sidestepped, Pastor Barnett said, "Brother Ron, tell us something. Talk to us." Then he looked at me again and said, "Wait a minute. Hold it...okay, Lord, I'll do that."

Suddenly Tommy Barnett picked up his Bible and removed his preaching outline from its pages. Then he handed me the Bible and said, "The Lord just said for you to preach." And then he walked off stage and disappeared!

I thought to myself while I stood in front of that huge crowd in Phoenix, *Now what kind of a revolting development is this? I don't want to preach. I don't want to be here!* Nevertheless, there I was, and all those people were looking at me. I just flipped open the Bible to my favorite verse of all time, Romans 8:28, and read, "And we know that all things work together for good to them that love God, to them who are the called according to His purpose."

I don't know what I said. I can't account for what came out of my mouth, but I do remember that within four minutes, no one was sitting in their seat anymore. They were standing and rejoicing in continuous praise. You could hear it like the sound of rolling water. God said something of incredible importance through me that night, and I still can't recall one word that I spoke! God just used this unwilling vessel to preach His Word—like a modern rendition of Balaam's ass.

After I preached, I went back to my seat and sat down—and immediately settled right back into my doldrums. I spent three days with Harvey, and I felt a lot better, at least. Then it was time to get back on the airplane.

Once again, my shrewd friend saw that the work wasn't done. "Do you know what, Pastor?" Harvey said. "I feel like just taking you back myself!" Then he canceled everything at his office, got on the airplane with me, and personally took me home.

He walked right into my living room with me (by this time, I guess he had had about enough), and sat down on the sofa. He said, "Pastor, I remember one time a preacher said that the only way you will ever get over a wrong being done to you and come into forgiveness is to pray in the Spirit for those who have wronged you."

"Harvey, I don't want to hear that," I said. I was the preacher he was quoting. He had heard me preach that message, and now my own sermon was coming back in my face. I said, "I don't want to hear that, Harvey. I just don't want to hear that." Unmoved, Harvey said, "Now, Pastor, we're going to pray." Then he stood up and walked over to my chair.

Harvey reached out and gently lifted me up out of my chair and stood me up in front of him so we were looking at one another eye to eye (like a little bitty seedling looks at a big, giant oak). Then he said, "We're going to pray, Pastor," as he grabbed both of my arms and started to kneel. Obviously, I went down to my knees too.

We were kneeling face to face, and tears started pouring from Harvey's eyes and falling on the carpet. I could see them falling on the knees of his pants. As he looked at me, I knew deep inside that he really loved me. He knew I was in trouble, and that I was hurting. He also knew I was about to let bitterness come in. This thing was about to make me bitter instead of better. It was about to become a *masuda* (a snare or trap) instead of a *masada* (fortress of strength). And Harvey saw it.

He started to pray as I listened. I was trying to be polite, and he wasn't really "getting to me" until he stopped praying. That is when he said, "Now, Pastor, this is the way you pray." Now I had two doctorate degrees, and this man was teaching me how to pray. He said, "This is the way you pray. Now say it after me, Pastor." I obediently started to repeat his words, and as I started to say them, they began to get into my heart ("For with the heart man believeth unto righteousness; and with the mouth confession is made unto salvation" [Romans 10:10]).

Harvey just prayed until he broke my heart, and pretty soon it started to come. The destiny was still in there. The design was still in there. And it started to rise as I yielded to God. It kept rising up until, after five minutes, my hands were in the air and tears were flowing as I prayed. Right then and there, the shackles of unforgiveness were broken off of my life and I was set free by the power of intercession for my enemies. It literally broke the bonds of unforgiveness and sin in my life. I stood up that day cleansed and whole, and Harvey went back home.

Forgiveness is a must. You have to cut a covenant. Two weeks after Harvey left, I was eating lunch at a hotel on Sunday with my wife, feeling wonderful, when I felt or sensed that someone was looking at me. There were about 400 people seated in that place, but I looked around and saw a tall, stately man standing across the room looking at me. It was the gentleman who had fired me.

He and I had enjoyed a great father-son relationship before the incident that drove us apart. He had been my "father in the Lord" before that, and *he loved me*. I'm sure he thought he had been right in doing what he did. I could see tears glistening in his eyes across the crowded, noisy room. He suddenly backed up from the table where his wife was seated on one side (a lady I will always love), and another friend I recognized on the other side. He went around three or four of his guests, stepped out in front of 500 people, and opened his arms with tears running down his face. (He *was* one of the greatest men I've ever known.) He was great, yet at the same time, he could cause great hurt. I knew him like few others knew him.

I embraced him, and we wept together in front of everyone. I forgave him and he forgave me. I experienced a bond that day that David must have had with Abner. A special bond of forgiving love seemed to melt the two of us together. After that day, I received some of the most kind and loving letters from that man.

I am saddened to say that within one year from that time, he was out of the office he had held, and within two years, he was in the grave. Yet I thank God that he and I were reconciled and that my life was set free by the power of forgiveness. The bondage between us was gone, and when he went to Heaven, he went to Heaven as my friend. It was all over. After all the years I had invested in it, my destiny would have stopped if it had not been for Harvey and the goodness of God. I "cut a covenant with forgiveness" that day, and I turned my *masuda* into a *masada*. I had learned a lesson. You can't take unforgiveness and hatred with you to Zion, or it will destroy you, and you will never achieve your destiny, your potential in God.

As for Harvey, he continued to become more prominent and became very wealthy. However, a few months later, Harvey was driving home and had a heart attack. He crashed his car into the wall and gates at his house and went to be with the Lord on the spot. Harvey is in Heaven today, and I will forever be grateful for his help, for he saved my life.

David learned the lesson of forgiveness when he cut a covenant with Abner. And after that lesson was complete, he had one more covenant to cut in Hebron. Perhaps the most sinister enemy of them all and the most difficult with which to walk in covenant is success and fame.

Paul wrote, *"Forgetting those things which are behind....* I press toward the mark for the prize of the high calling of God in Christ Jesus" (Phil. 3:13b-14). This was Paul's journey to Zion. Paul had to "forget" a whole lot more than his sins and his sacrifices to reach the prize. We may want to look at our accomplishments and say, "Oh, but look at what I've given up. Look at how wonderful and special I am." God says, "Forget those things which are behind."

What have you and I given up, after all? "Well, I gave up a good job making a bunch of money." You could "keep" it and then try to take that to Heaven with you.... If you are alive and well 100 years from now, talk with the people in that day about the sacrifice you made 100 years earlier. Who is going to care whether you made $500,000 a year or $5,000 a year? The truth is, nothing we give up will really last beyond the grave.

Paul had to forget his successes as well as his sins. This man had been successful in Judaism. He said, "And [I] profited in the Jews' religion above many my equals in mine own nation, being more exceedingly zealous of the traditions of my fathers" (Gal. 1:14).

It is my belief that if Paul had remained in Judaism, he would have been "the next Gamaliel," replacing his famous teacher as chief rabbi. First came Hillel, generally considered the greatest rabbi of all time, and Gamaliel's teacher. Then came Gamaliel, who was Paul's teacher. Paul said he was "…brought up in this city [Jerusalem] at the feet of Gamaliel, and taught according to the perfect manner of the law of the fathers, and was zealous toward God…" (Acts 22:3).

Perhaps he would have become the next leader of Judaism in his day. Now that was "success" according to the standards of men. Paul was a successful man in Judaism, but he "forgot" all that. Long before Paul's day, David also faced the challenge of cutting a covenant with success and fame.

Then came all the tribes of Israel to David unto Hebron, and spake, saying, Behold, we are thy bone and thy flesh. Also in time past, when Saul was king over us, thou wast he that leddest out and broughtest in Israel: and the Lord said to thee, Thou shalt feed My people Israel, and thou shalt be a captain over Israel. So all the elders of Israel came to the king to Hebron; and king David made a league with them in Hebron before the Lord: and they anointed David king over Israel (2 Samuel 5:1-3).

David had to cut a covenant with his own successful destiny. When you read about the elders of Israel coming to David in Hebron, didn't you wonder, *Where have these wonderful people been for the past 14 years? Where were they when David was scrambling for his life in Adullam? Where were they during the years he was ruling in Judah and battling with Abner?* They were there all the time. They saw the rising tide of divine destiny in David, and everyone knew that God had anointed him king in Israel—yet they did nothing to aid him or recognize his divine destiny.

The very day Saul died, they should have headed straight for David and recognized him as king of Israel. Instead, they allowed Abner to hoodwink them. They allowed David to be horribly and maliciously mistreated so they could continue to "feather their own nests," save their own hides, and keep their own positions. Now Saul was dead. Right after Abner cut a covenant with David, he was murdered by Joab in revenge for the death of a brother, leaving Ishbosheth and all Israel without a "strong man" to protect them.

Saul was dead, Abner was dead, and Saul's son, Ishbosheth, was soon murdered in his bed by two of his own captains. Even the stubborn elders of Israel had to recognize that they couldn't stop the divine destiny of God in the life of David. This is important: No one can stop the divine destiny for your life either—no one but you. In the end, the elders of Israel had to come before the shepherd God had chosen and ask for a covenant.

It would have been easy for David to say, "I'm sorry, what are your names again? I believe I have forgotten who you are [as you forgot me]." David was in charge at this point. He had the army. He had the hearts of the people. And David had God's blessing. Now these leaders needed him, but only a few days before they would have refused to come to him, even though he needed them.

David could have said, "No, I don't believe I need you at this point. Why don't all of you resign right now." His army could have taken Israel by force—there was no question about it. Israel didn't have a king or an "emerging leader" of any kind. David could have squashed them if he had wanted to. Now these people, "from the wrong side of the tracks," were knocking at his door, asking him, "Make a league with us, David."

How would you feel if these men came to you and said, "Behold, we are thy bone and thy flesh" (2 Sam. 5:1b), after they had sided with your enemies for seven and one-half years? These men were absolute hypocrites. They conveniently "forgot" those years and jumped all the way back to the time when David was "Mr. Popular" in Israel, the man who had destroyed Goliath. They said, "Also in time past, when Saul was king over us, thou wast he that leddest out and broughtest in Israel: and the Lord said to thee, Thou shalt feed My people Israel, and thou shalt be a captain over Israel" (2 Sam. 5:2). These hypocrites condemned themselves by confirming that they knew all about David's calling and destiny from the beginning! Now they had the gall to use the words of God out of context, yet it was all within the divine destiny of God for David. Why? David had another covenant to establish, another lesson to learn.

There is a deep irony in the verse that says "...all the elders of Israel came to the king *to Hebron*" (2 Sam. 5:3a). This is magnificent! Look at what God did for David.

When David should have rightfully been offered the throne of Israel, the elders and their general wouldn't let him enter Jerusalem in Israel. What did God do? He brought "all the tribes of Israel" and "all the elders of Israel" to David in lowly Hebron! Oh, that's just wonderful. If it hasn't sunk in yet, it is time to understand that God will fulfill your destiny, and the only person who can stop it is you!

The Bible says, "King David made a league with them in Hebron before the Lord [Yahweh]: and they anointed David king over Israel" (2 Sam. 5:3b). Now, when these tribal elders came to David he cut a covenant with them and forgave them. He did this even though they had ignored and snubbed him for seven and one-half years during his reign as king of Judah as well as the seven and one-half years before that he had spent at the cave of Adullam. David acted as though these wrongs had never even happened. He didn't go through any of the trauma that I went through, because he quickly forgave and forgot the past.

It was at this point of David's ascendancy that I believe he was most vulnerable to temptation and sin. The moment everything seemed to be going his way, he *could have* just raised his eyebrow or written a royal decree to depose this enemy, overthrow that one, or undermine this other one. He could have done anything that he wanted to do, yet he did none of these things. He forgave his enemies and accepted them as friends. Incredible! These are the actions of a man after God's own heart, a man who has cut three vital covenants in Hebron: a covenant with failure, a covenant with forgiveness, and finally, a covenant with success and fame.

Let's summarize up to this point. We have gone through three classrooms, clearinghouses, or supply stations, on the road to Zion (our destiny). All three of these classrooms are necessary, and each has three lessons to be learned. First, we visited Bethlehem, the place of calling, anointing, and beginning. We learned about spiritual authority by finding a "king to serve." We learned personal integrity by finding "a giant to kill." And we learned personal intimacy by finding "a friend to love."

The second classroom was Adullam, a place of testing, learning, and growing. The lesson of compassion learned here taught us to accept people for their needs, not ours. The lesson of courage taught us to be willing to lay down our life for others at the call of God. The lesson of character showed us that "the ends do not justify the means"; the will of God is never contrary to the character of God.

Finally, David led us to Hebron—the place of commitment, relationship, and covenant. We learned with David how to "fall forward in failure," and we learned the costly lesson of forgiveness. Finally, we learned how to keep success in proper balance. These are the three classrooms and the nine lessons of David's course of training for reigning.

Now let us move ahead to possess our destiny by seizing our spiritual birthright. There are five steps involved.

Chapter 8

Five Steps to Zion

David had been crowned king of Israel, but he had one "small" problem: He was still sitting on a throne in Hebron. His destiny didn't end in Judah; his road led northward to Mount Zion, the site of Israel's ancient capital, Jerusalem. It wasn't necessarily an easy road, but it was the path of destiny. Zion is the place of reigning, of fullness, and of destiny.

And the king and his men went to Jerusalem unto the Jebusites, the inhabitants of the land: which spake unto David, saying, Except thou take away the blind and the lame, thou shalt not come in hither: thinking, David cannot come in hither (2 Samuel 5:6).

David was ready and poised to go up to Zion. The Bible says that when the king and his men went to Jerusalem to talk with the Jebusites who inhabited the land, the Jebusites taunted and mocked David and his army, saying, "We're going to fight you with our blind people and with our lame people because that's all we're going to need to keep you out. You can't get in here. Nobody has ever taken this fortress."

The original name of ancient Jerusalem was "Jebus," and it was inhabited by the Jebusites. Nobody had ever conquered this group descended from the tribe of Benjamin. They lived in a fortress or fort on Mount Zion that had the reputation of being virtually impregnable. That is why these men impudently bragged that their blind and lame men could repel David's army.

This was the very tribe from which Saul was descended. Of course you remember that David used a sling to bring Goliath down. In the time of Jacob, the people of Benjamin were known as "the left-handed slingers" who had won renown in the army of Israel for their ability to throw stones out of slingshots with remarkable accuracy. If that was Saul's heritage, then David fought Goliath the way Saul *should* have been fighting him! Unfortunately, Saul had long since given up fighting the way he should have as a son of Benjamin. Instead, Saul chose to fight like a Philistine. Isn't that incredible?

> *Nevertheless David took the strong hold of Zion: the same is the city of David. And David said on that day, Whosoever getteth up to the gutter, and smiteth the Jebusites, and the lame and the blind, that are hated of David's soul, he shall be chief and captain. Wherefore they said, The blind and the lame shall not come into the house* (2 Samuel 5:7-8).

David evidently removed Joab from his position as the captain of David's hosts because he murdered Abner (see 2 Sam. 3:27-39). When David announced that he would make "whoever gets up there first" the general of his army, Joab's ears perked up. The reason David was out there leading this battle himself was because he didn't have a general. Joab must have asked David, "Does that include me?" You know what happened after that. Joab was the first man over the wall and into the city. He personally saw to it that David's army took that "impregnable fortress" and he was immediately reinstated as the general of David's army.

*Nevertheless David **took** the strong hold of Zion: the same is the city of David ... So David **dwelt** in the fort, and called it the city of David. And David **built** round about from Millo and inward. And David **went on**, and grew great, and the Lord God of hosts (was) with him* (2 Samuel 5:7,9-10).

(I have made some of the words in the Scripture passage bold to make them stand out to you, and the word in parentheses is marked to show that it doesn't belong there—it isn't in the original manuscript.)

Training alone will not automatically hand you your destiny on a silver platter. You can be "ready" and still miss your destiny! Why? Qualifications and readiness are essential, but the only way to fulfill your destiny is to reach out and take hold of it when God brings you to your Zion. You have to assert yourself in it to fully possess it. There are five steps that must be taken to capture your throne in Zion.

Step 1: Put your body where your destiny is.

David put his body where his destiny was when he went to Jerusalem. It took him 14 years from the time he fled Jerusalem for his life, but the Bible says, "And the king and his men went to Jerusalem unto the Jebusites, the inhabitants of the land..." (2 Sam. 5:6). David put his body where his calling was. He changed his environment to assure that he would remain destiny-conscious and destiny-focused. I've lost count of the number of people I've heard say, "God has called me to be a minister," or "God has called me to go to Africa," or "God has called me to go to China," or simply, "God has called me." Why haven't these people ever done what they are called to do? It is because they failed to "put their bodies where their calling was." They were stuck in a rut, self-confined in an environment that was not conducive to the establishment of their lives and ministries.

I went through Bible college with a fellow who used to say to everyone around him each day, "If I miss Africa, I'll miss Heaven!" In those days, the way to win an appointment to the mission field was to graduate from Bible school and then put in two years of active ministry in the states. This young man married a girl he met in Bible school, and they both intended to go to the mission field. After they graduated, he pastored a church for two years. And all along the way he kept telling everyone, "If I miss Africa, I'll miss Heaven."

While he was out itinerating among the churches to raise money for his trip to Africa, he went into a restaurant where he was served by an attractive waitress who evidently caught his eye. He wound up running off with the waitress and leaving behind his poor wife (and his favorite phrase—"If I miss Africa, I'll miss Heaven").

This man's wife went on to Africa alone, but he never made it. I can still remember the nights he used to wake me up in the Bible college dormitory as he prayed while half-asleep, "Africa. Africa." I'd say, "Go to sleep," and a few minutes later he would murmur again, "Africa." He was serious at that point in his life, but something happened. He ran off with a waitress, putting his body where his "falling" was instead of where his calling was.

God will ultimately bring you to a point where you either "put up or you shut up."

David's destiny kept him from wasting his time, interest, and energy on trivial things and "flesh-feeding" diversions. "But I have to make this money first. Let me work for another ten years and make this money...then I'll head for Zion." Yeah, you might wind up running off with someone too. "I have to have a little fun first. I want to 'live a little' first. I'll give myself to the work of God, but first of all, I want to go to Tahiti." My flesh-feeding diversions are too demanding for me to think about Zion. "I don't like studying. I usually watch television until one o'clock in the morning—it's my way of relaxing. You know how it is." No, these things are flesh-feeding diversions.

Put your body where your calling is. It takes discipline, and it isn't easy, but if you ever once know the joy of flowing free in your destiny, you will never settle for second-best. If you ever experience the thrill of realizing that the anointing in your ministry isn't coming from your mind or from your mouth, but from the deepest recesses of your spiritual being—you will feel "in sync" with the God of this universe! You will feel and know that you are a vital part of God's purpose in the earth. If you ever have this experience, *nothing else will ever satisfy you*!

David had experienced a touch of this. It was so unforgettable that he literally pushed aside all the power, prestige, popularity, fun, money, and pride that was offered to him apart from God's plan. David steadfastly put his body where his calling was in spite of the obvious risks attached to his obedience.

This concept of "destiny focus" is perfectly illustrated in the story of Nehemiah's stand for God in the midst of his enemies:

Now it came to pass, when Sanballat, and Tobiah, and Geshem the Arabian, and the rest of our enemies, heard that I had builded the wall [of Jerusalem], *and that there was no breach left* [in the wall]; *(though at that time I had not set up the doors upon the gates;) that Sanballat and Geshem sent unto me, saying, Come, let us meet together in some one of the villages in the plain of Ono. But they thought to do me mischief* (Nehemiah 6:1-2).

This ancient leader was an Old Testament "apostle." He knew his enemies wanted to do him mischief. They hoped to kill him once they got him away from the fortified city and the people. These men were the leaders of the Samaritans, and they weren't happy that God had sent Nehemiah back to Jerusalem to rebuild the city and its walls, and to reestablish the kingdom in Israel.

Nehemiah's reply was blunt and to the point: "And I sent messengers unto them, saying, I am doing a great work, so that I cannot come down: why should the work cease, whilst I leave it, and come down to you?" (Neh. 6:3) He was saying, "Don't invite me to come to any kind of summit for heads of state: I am too busy fulfilling my destiny. I'm too involved in God's project to discuss yours."

The late C.M. Ward preached on the "Revivaltime" radio program for 25 years, and he was probably as responsible as any other individual for the current renewal going on today in the Church of Jesus Christ. I heard Brother Ward say, "Bless God, I'm a preacher. Don't invite me to be president of your United States. I don't have time for such trivia—I'm a preacher. I can't be your senator. I'm not interested in your United Nations, I don't have time for foolishness. I'm a preacher, and I'm on the wall." I believe that is what David felt. He was on his way to his destiny, and he didn't have time for anything else.

This kind of confidence and focus on one goal reminds me of the cellist who persistently played one note in the orchestra while everybody else's fingers were flying. The others noticed this fellow sawing away at his one note, and they asked him, "Sir, why don't you play something else?" He confidently replied, "Why should I? I've found the note, and all the rest of you are still searching!"

When you find the note of God for your life, play that note with all of your strength and energy. When you find who you are and what you are in Christ, play that note for life. God will let others find their notes and blend in with you to bring the harmony. Your job is to *play your note*! I love to see a prophet who *is* a prophet. I may not like him, but I love him. He may "rub my fur" the wrong way with some of the things he thinks and says, but I want him to *be a prophet*, not a makeshift clone of someone else. God will help me in my apostolic calling to blend in this prophet's ministry with that of the evangelists, teachers, and pastors/shepherds so all will function together as a harmonious whole. Just play your note like David played his.

Another great example of "destiny focus" is found in the Book of Matthew:

Now when Jesus saw great multitudes about Him, He gave commandment to depart unto the other side. And a certain scribe came, and said unto Him, Master, I will follow Thee whithersoever Thou goest. And Jesus saith unto him, The foxes have holes, and the birds of the air have nests; but the Son of man hath not where to lay His head (Matthew 8:18-20).

This passage says a certain "scribe" came to Jesus and offered to follow Jesus wherever He went. The Greek word for "scribe," *grammateus*, means "scholar or professional writer." This man was a biblical scholar of the first order, an acknowledged scribe. This is a man who had the responsibility of transcribing the sacred law of his nation and God. The scribes were the "brain trusts" of Israel.

Consider what Jesus said to him: "Foxes have holes, and the birds of the air have nests; but the Son of man hath not where to lay His head." Jesus said this knowing that Israel took good care of its scribes. Even in modern Israel, the scribes are considered to be a separate and highly-honored culture of people. Most of these scribes come from a small sect of so-called "black Jews," a term drawn from their black clothing. The Israeli state actually supports these highly paid scribes, and they live in the most expensive areas, the "Beverly Hills" of Jerusalem.

One time on one of our tours I booked a group of people into a five-star hotel in Jerusalem. During the stay, I stepped into an open elevator and punched the elevator button for my floor, but the elevator car wouldn't work. Then a family of Jews totally dressed in black walked into the elevator. The man said to me, "Out, out. This is our elevator." I found out that the elevator I was in was reserved only for these people, and it would only go to the top two floors, which were also reserved for scribes. Everyone else had to use the public elevator and stay in the bottom three floors.

This was the kind of man who had come to Jesus. The Lord was reminding this scholar and church official, "I don't have anywhere to lay My head. I want to remind you, son, that you've been living in the lap of luxury. Now, if you're going to follow Me, you will have some problems." If you look closely, the Bible does not say that the man actually followed Jesus after that.

And another of His disciples said unto Him, Lord, suffer me first to go and bury my father. But Jesus said unto him, Follow Me; and let the dead bury their dead (Matthew 8:21-22).

Jesus was telling this man, "You will have to give up all this stuff and count it but dung and trivia. Put your body where your calling is." (See also Philippians 3:8.) This is where "the rubber meets the road." You can preach and shout and have a great time, but until you make these kinds of decisions, you really won't fulfill the divine destiny God planted inside of you. This is the kind of commitment Paul made.

When David got to Zion, he discovered that his inheritance, the capital city of Israel, was already occupied by the Jebusites, descendants of Israel's ancient enemies, the Canaanites and Amorites. The ancient name for Jerusalem, *Jebus*, means "trampled down, burned over, and dried up." Jebus was trampled down, burned over, and dried up. Now look closely at this Scripture passage:

And the children of Benjamin did not drive out the Jebusites that inhabited Jerusalem; but the Jebusites dwell with the children of Benjamin in Jerusalem unto this day (Judges 1:21).

The Jebusites represented about the same thing that Goliath represented—demon spirits, strongholds, the old nature, and tradition. David was facing yet another Goliath threatening to prevent his destiny. It is time for us to face a great truth about this life: "Anything worthwhile in the Kingdom will have to be taken out of enemy hands!"

You and I live in this carnal flesh, surrounded by a world system filled with hindrances. We know we have a divine destiny, but that destiny will have to be taken away from the enemy. God called Abraham and told him, "And I will give unto thee, and to thy seed after thee, the land wherein thou art a stranger, all the land of Canaan, for an everlasting possession; and I will be their God" (Gen. 17:8).

Just as the descendants of Abraham had to take their inheritance away from their enemies, you too will face giants in the land of your destiny. Your inheritance belongs to you. It is your birthright. But you will never inherit your birthright unless you *take* it.

When David went to the Jebusites after arriving in Jerusalem, they just mocked him and his men. In their pride and devilish presumption about the invincibility of their fortress, they bragged to the man of God, "You can't come in here. We don't care what God has said. You say you know it's yours, but you're not strong enough to take it. You can't even defeat the blind and lame among us!" Demon spirits do that to believers every day. In fact, your carnal nature and religious tradition do the same thing. You have to break these things down to possess your inheritance.

Step 2: Don't reason with the enemy—*take what is yours*!

The Bible says, "*Nevertheless*, David **took** the stronghold of Zion" (2 Sam. 5:7a). This is the same way you and I should *take* what belongs to us as God's sons and daughters and as joint heirs with Jesus Christ. When we find that our inheritance is inhabited by Jebusites, or "giants in the land" (Canaan is full of giants like demon spirits, our carnal nature, religious tradition, and many others), we need to refuse to reason with the enemy. We need to just *take what is ours*.

David did not bother to answer or reason with the Jebusites. He ignored their taunting words and just took back what was his. The enemy has stolen your destiny and hedged around it so that you can't get to it. I've heard a lot of people say, "Well, brother, you have to learn the name of a demon before you can deal with it." I'm sorry, but I'm not interested in knowing some foul demon's name. I refuse to make him my friend or engage in any kind of social intercourse with him whatsoever. I'll just say, "Hey you, get out of the way! In Jesus' name, get out!" You don't need to have a conversation, hold court, or share a social discourse with Jebusites—just knock them down and take back what belongs to you.

Don't argue with them. Zion is your birthright. Your destiny is yours. You've caught a glimpse of it. You've felt a touch of the anointing. You've come to understand what life can be when up out of your innermost being flow rivers of living water. You've experienced a taste of Zion, so don't be deterred. Take possession of what is yours.

The Hebrew language actually has two words for "inherit." The first Hebrew term translated as "inherit" or "inheritance" in the Old Testament is the legal term, *nachalah*. It means "something inherited, as an estate, awarded as a legal heritage or possession." The Greek equivalent of this word is *exsousia*, which means "authority." Jesus said, "All [authority, *exsousia*] is given unto Me in heaven and in earth" (Mt. 28:18b), and "Behold, I give unto you power [*Exsousia*] to tread on serpents and scorpions, and over all the power [*Dunimus*; the enemy has power, but no authority] of the enemy: and nothing shall by any means hurt you [take away your right relationship with God]" (Lk. 10:19).

You and I have authority, but the problem is we must *take* it. The second Hebrew word for "inherit," *yarash*, is an "action" word, while *nachalah* is the legal term describing a "thing." *Nachalah* means "authority," while *yarash* means "ability." The Greek equivalent of *yarash* is *ischuos*, which means "I can." It refers to the ability to do a thing. Paul declared, "I can do [*ischuos*] all things through Christ which strengtheneth me" (Phil. 4:13).

The Hebrew term, *yarash*, is a little stronger than its Greek equivalent. It means "to occupy by driving out previous tenants." There it is. You have a *nachalah*, or an inheritance and birthright through Christ Jesus. But like David faced with the jeering Jebusites up in their fortified city, the day will come when you will have to *yarash* or "seize, take possession and control of" your destiny as God's child.

In biblical truth, Canaan is your birthright. The Kingdom is your birthright, but it is populated by giants. Like David of old, you must *take* it away from Jebusites and giants; you have to seize it by force. You need to "*yarash* your *nachalah*."

I heard a preacher tell a story about a tax collector who came to a farm to serve a legal document and seize a farmer's property for unpaid taxes. When he came up to the house, the farmer's wife knew that legal document had to be served on the one who had legally signed the ownership papers on the property, so she said, "I don't know anything about this. You'll have to go and talk to my husband about it."

"Do you see my husband way across that field over there?" she asked. When he had some trouble seeing her husband in the distance, she said, "Do you see that big fence? Well, he's working way on the other side of that field. You'll have to serve the paper on him."

The tax collector frowned and said, "Well, how do I get there?" She answered, "I guess you'll have to go across that field." Well, the tax collector took his legal paper in hand and headed toward the fence to cross the field. Since the fence was pretty high and difficult to negotiate, especially in office attire, it took him several minutes to clear the fence. This revenuer was sporting a big red tie and a red shirt. Right about the time he was halfway across that field, he heard a snort. He looked over to his right and saw the biggest, meanest, ugliest, and maddest bull he had ever seen in his life! Suddenly that bull started chasing him, and he began to run for his life, screaming at the top of his voice. The farmer's wife saw the whole thing, and she stepped out on the porch and cupped her hands to her mouth to shout to the man, "Show him the papers, mister. Show him the papers!"

Legal papers don't amount to much if you can't serve them, do they? Your heavenly Father has bought anything and everything you will ever need, and He's paid the price in full with the blood of Jesus Christ, His only begotten Son. The only way to collect this inheritance is to "stamp it" with your own faith and reach out for your destiny to possess it. You have to *yarash* your *nachalah*!

When God told Abraham, "...I am the Lord that brought thee out of Ur of the Chaldees, to give thee this land to *inherit it*" (Gen. 15:7), He was saying "I gave you this land [this inheritance] to *yarash*, or seize, and take possession of it!"

This didn't happen until Joshua came along many years later. Israel struggled to possess the land for many years, and then the people rested for a time. Finally God spoke to Joshua:

> *Now Joshua was old and stricken in years; and the Lord said unto him, Thou art old and stricken in years, and*

there remaineth yet very much land to be possessed (Joshua 13:1).

How can people say the Bible doesn't have humor in it? How would you like for God to tell you, "Well, you're old and rickety now..."? God was saying, "Joshua, there is still a lot of land (your inheritance) to be *yarashed* (seized)."

Then God said, "All the inhabitants of the hill country from Lebanon unto Misrephothmaim, and all the Sidonians, them will I drive out from before the children of Israel: only divide thou it by lot unto the Israelites for an inheritance, as I have commanded thee" (Josh. 13:6). Once again, the term "drive out" in this verse is *yarash*.

God also told His leader that the way to handle the mammoth job of helping all of Israel to seize [*yarash*] their inheritance was to divide the inheritance [*nachalah*] by lot among them. This is a picture of the primary purpose of ministry in the New Testament church. The ministers of God are to help people discover their *nachalah*, their birthright in God, and then teach and motivate them to *yarash*, or seize and possess, their inheritance in Christ. Isaiah used this same pair of words in the same way in Isaiah 57:13.

If you put your trust in God, you will *receive your birthright*, and God will help you *seize* it out of enemy hands. So we must not only put our bodies where our calling is, we must also *take* our birthright away from the enemy. (Remember, "the enemy" is not people, but the principalities and powers, and rulers of the darkness of this world and wicked spirits in the heavens [see Eph. 6:12].)

Step 3: Dwell in your destiny and call it yours!

*So David **dwelt** in the fort, and **called** it the city of David. And David built round about from Millo and inward. And David went on, and grew great, and the Lord God of hosts was with him* (2 Samuel 5:9-10).

David *dwelt* in the fort (*masada*) his army had captured. This Hebrew word means "a fastness, castle, defense, fortress, stronghold, and strong place." David used this *masada* as his dwelling place. This man's experiences on his journey to Zion became his *masada*, even more powerful and secure than the fortified city he had just seized from the descendants of giants, the Jebusites. David was now "dwelling" in his destiny.

There are two things involved with "dwelling" in your destiny: ruling and confessing. "So David *dwelt* in the fort, and *called* it the city of David." The word *dwelt* comes from the Hebrew word *yashab*. This word doesn't mean to just "hang around." *Yashab* means "to seat oneself, to take the proper seat."

It means "to find your place, your seat, and your rightful destiny in the Kingdom of God." Every one of us has his own unique, divine design from God. When each of us finds his place in the Body, then we will have wholeness. Every high throne of authority in the Kingdom of God begins as a humble seat of servanthood in the Church. Reach out and take that destiny through servanthood. Seat yourself in your destiny and dwell in it as David dwelt in his. David "*yasab*'ed" in his *matsadah*. He sat down in his ordained place and authority, to dwell in his destiny, his fortress. The wanderer, the shepherd of roving flocks, the captain of a vagabond army on the run, had changed his lifestyle forever. He settled himself into his destiny and prepared to "stay put" for life.

David wrote these lovely words:

Behold, how good and how pleasant it is for brethren to dwell together in unity! It is like the precious ointment [shemin, anointing oil] upon the head, that ran down upon the beard, even Aaron's beard: that ran down to the skirts [peh-mouth] of his garments; as the dew of Hermon, and as the dew that descended upon the mountains of Zion: for there the Lord commanded the blessing, even life for evermore (Psalm 133:1-3).

The New Testament parallel to the Hebrew word *yashab* appears in Luke 24:49 and in the Book of Matthew. Just as Jesus was getting ready to go back to Heaven, He said, "...Behold, I send the promise of My Father upon you: but *tarry* ye in the city of Jerusalem, until ye be endued with power from on high" (Lk. 24:49). The Greek word for "tarry" is *kathizo*.

Then I remembered the passage in Matthew's Gospel where Jesus *took His seat* and gave His followers the by-laws of the Kingdom, the Beatitudes and the Sermon on the Mount. The Greek word used here for "seated" is *kathizomai*. It comes from *kathizo*. I thought, "Could it be?" The definition for *kathizo* was identical to that of the Hebrew word *yashab*. *Jesus took His seat as King in the new Kingdom and in His destiny.* Then He opened His mouth and out of Him poured the living water of the Sermon on the Mount, establishing the new covenant and the new Kingdom.

When David came into his destiny and seated himself in Zion, he enthroned himself in his destiny. When he came to understand it everything else came into a balance and wholeness because he was totally focused on who and what he was in God. He established himself there.

Jesus had instructed the disciples to *tarry*, or wait, until they received the promise of the Father. The passage in the Book of Acts that describes how the 120 were endued with power in the Holy Spirit begins, "And *suddenly* there came a sound from heaven as of a rushing mighty wind, and it filled all the house where they were sitting" (Acts 2:2).

Why did things happen "suddenly"? I believe the key is in the first verse of that chapter: "And when the day of Pentecost was fully come, they were all with *one accord* in *one place*." Each believer was in one place and one accord in the Body. Each person filled his or her destined place in the Body of Christ. That is when the Bible says, "Suddenly" God poured out His Spirit. God is still the same today.

When the Church gets in order, God will pour out His blessing just as suddenly. We say we want a harvest and we want revival. Well, all we have to do is come into destined order. Once we find out who we are, where we belong, and get into proper order, then revival will come. God was ready a long time ago: As usual, He is waiting on us!

The second part of dwelling is *confessing*. David called Jerusalem the "city of David." The Hebrew word for "called" is *qara*. This word also appears in Genesis 1:5; 1:8; 1:10 and so on, when God "called" into being everything that was not! God *called* for light, and He *called* for day. God *called* for the fishes, and He *called* for the trees. God called the universe into being. Its Greek equivalent appears in Romans 4:17, in which the apostle Paul declares:

*(As it is written, I have made thee a father of many nations,) before Him whom he believed, even God, who quickeneth the dead, and **calleth** [kaleo] those things which be not as though they were.*

The Hebrew word *qara* and the Greek word *kaleo* both mean "to call out of nothingness into being." David sat down in his seat of authority and destiny and boldly called Jerusalem "my city." He said, "This is my town because it is my destiny in God." It depresses me to fly into a city to preach only to hear my host pastor run down the very place where God has planted him. "This is the worst city in the state. We have the lousiest economy, the lousiest mayor, and the lousiest city council. People here are just no good, they are worthless bums...blah, blah, blah." This type of pastor will fail. He is absolutely going to fail. Jeremiah reminded us that even if we find ourselves in Babylon we should pray for the place where God has placed us (see Jer. 29:7). You may not approve of everything about it, but just get in there and get involved to make it better.

Every time I go to Israel, I go to the ancient fortress called Masada, where ancient Israel made a last stand against the Roman legions. Masada is still a place of induction into the Israeli army. It is where new soldiers take the pledge of allegiance to the country of Israel. Every group that is inducted into the army declares aloud, "Masada, Masada" (which means, of course, "ordained, set, established, my place in Israel"). I think we need something like this in the Church.

Invest yourself in your destiny. David called Jerusalem "my city." You call your Jerusalem "my ministry."

Say, "This is my church," and "These are my elders," or "That is my pastor." Declare out loud, "If that child misses God and goes to hell, I'm responsible," or "I have been entrusted with this by eldership. This is my calling; I'm appointed. God has put me here, and the angels of Heaven, the hosts of Heaven, stand ready to help me." You should be able to say with confidence, "This is my destiny; I'm established."

Step 4: Restructure your priorities.

The Bible says, "So David dwelt in the fort, and called it the city of David. And David built round about from Millo and inward" (2 Sam. 5:9). The fourth step in capturing your destiny is epitomized by David, who "built *round about* from Millo and inward."

The Hebrew word for "build" is *banah*. It means "to repair and strengthen and set up." David rebuilt and repaired everything around him, especially around the center of his destiny. *Millo* means "a filled in rampart, citadel, or headquarters." Millo became David's royal briefing room, the heart of the fortress of Jerusalem. Millo represented the heart of the city. This is where David heard from God and conferred with his leaders. Everything David did was built around Millo as a center, which represents the disciplined life. He built and ordered his life around his destiny. He determined what he did each day in terms of who he was in God.

> You don't fit divine destiny into your current lifestyle. Don't try to make God accommodate you. You accommodate God!

I remember hearing of the time some friends of the painter James Whistler bought one of his great works of art for display in a gallery in their home. They took the painting home and tried to mount it in their gallery, but it didn't seem to fit in anywhere. It seemed to be awkward. This couple got in touch with their friend, the great artist, and said, "What are we going to do? We can't fit this great work of art into our gallery." Whistler simply replied, "The answer to that, sir, is simple. Destroy the gallery and rebuild it."

Some of us must destroy our old lifestyle and rebuild it around the center of our God-given destiny. Allow the wind of God's Spirit to blow away anything extraneous. Use the sharp sword of His living Word to cut away elements that do not belong.

Step 5: Keep on and grow great with God.

David put his body where his calling was. He took his birthright out of enemy hands and dwelt in it. He enthroned himself in it, and he called it his own. He restructured his priorities to conform to his destiny in God. Then the Bible says, "And David went on, and grew great, and the Lord God of hosts was with him" (2 Sam. 5:10).

David's task was to make this his lifestyle. When the Bible says, "He went on," it means David made ruling within his destiny his *lifestyle*. David's destiny and purpose was to sit, to nest, to enthrone himself in his divine calling. David just wasn't interested in anything contrary to his calling (whenever he *did* stray from this, he got into terrible trouble).

I have a saying posted on my wall where I can see it from my desk. I look at it every day. It says, "The main thing is to keep the main thing the main thing." There are all kinds of distractions, all kinds of camels that want to get their noses under your tent. If you let them in, pretty soon there won't be any room for anything else. David kept everything in its place, and he kept his destiny at the center of his life. He disciplined his life around his destiny.

David's task was to keep on, pursue, go forward, and make his God-given destiny a lifestyle. God's task after that is "automatic." He just keeps blessing! I have a definition for greatness that you might want to write down: *"Greatness is conformity to destiny."* You are a unique fingerprint of God. There is only one of you in the earth, and you are awesome. You are marvelous in His sight. You are an instrument of His grace as nobody else can be.

If you want to become great like David, then just become that divine fingerprint of God in the earth. Become the destiny that God ordained and designed before the foundation of the world. That is greatness. Anything short of it is not "great." Whether you become a movie star earning $7 million per motion picture or build the modern equivalent of the Taj Mahal, if it is not conformity to your destiny, then it's failure. Greatness is conformity to the divine design in your day-by-day activity. And the Bible says, "And David...grew great, and *the Lord God of hosts [was] with him*" (2 Sam. 5:10). If you remember my earlier comment, the word "was" isn't in the original text. The original text literally says, "And David grew great, and the Lord grew great with him"! If you are fully centered on Him, then He will make you great. He does this so that *through you and in you*, He will be made great in your life and in the lives of others.

Chapter 9

Prepare for Revival

Why was God so intent on getting David into Zion? Why did He work from before the foundation of the world to implant such a divine design and destiny in David? The answer is this: God helped David overcome every obstacle because He knew that if He brought David to Zion, then David would bring *Him* to Zion too. God loved Israel, and He wanted to deliver Israel through David.

What was the first thing David did when he came into Zion? He immediately recovered the ark of the covenant and took steps to restore it to its proper place in the heart of Zion. If you dare to pledge your life to bringing the presence of God into your world, then God will dedicate Himself to bringing you into your destiny!

After David's training for reigning was complete and he had taken Zion, David immediately prepared for revival in Israel. The first step is very interesting: "And Hiram king of Tyre sent messengers to David, and cedar trees, and carpenters, and masons: *and they built David an house*" (2 Sam. 5:11).

David immediately established permanent residence in Zion. Some time ago I learned that in the leading Evangelical and Pentecostal denominations, the average length of stay in a pastorate is 22 months! Now how can you be a spiritual father to anyone in 22 months? All you're doing is raising bastard children who struggle to grow up without a spiritual father! They're not yours; they're not even someone else's; they are fatherless (*orphanos*, see John 14:18). You will spend all your time (22 months) trying to understand *who* they are first (because they don't know—they don't know their father) before you can ever influence *what* they are. There are many great pastors in these denominations, but I can't condone any system that moves ministers around to keep their ultimate loyalty to a system instead of to the Lord and to the sheep He entrusts to them.

David established permanent residency in Zion. It will give you a great deal of strength and authority as a spiritual leader when you know God has sovereignly planted you in a place for the "long haul." You're not going to get voted out or chased off. You will be there when they come and when they go. God establishes and plants His servants so they can sink deep roots and bear much fruit to His glory. The fly-by-night "here today, gone tomorrow" system is man's doing.

It's interesting that David didn't build his house—the people did. It is important for every man and woman of God to have a permanent place in Zion. A few years back, people began to realize that God was restoring the gift of apostles to the Church. All of a sudden, a lot of people who saw themselves as apostles felt they had to resign their local churches to become missionaries (the old definition of apostle)—"like Paul." This only demonstrated our ignorance concerning Paul's life and ministry, as well as the biblical definition of an apostle. Paul was always in direct relationship with a home church! He always went out from that home church base (Acts 13:4; 15:30) and came back to that home church base (Acts 14:26; 18:22). Antioch was Paul's base, although he became very closely related to the Galatians, the Ephesians, and then the Philippians. Antioch was Paul's home church. He always had his feet planted firmly in a local church.

Thank God, true apostles are now recognizing their vital need and biblical mandate to have a permanent local base. They can't just be "floaters" any more than anyone else. There is no such gifting as "missionary" in the Bible. Even our classic picture of the "missionary" who plants churches in foreign nations and cultures has been firmly rooted in a local base, with accountability to that local base. That's the way apostolic ministry works.

And Hiram king of Tyre sent messengers to David, and cedar trees, and carpenters, and masons: and they built David an house. And David perceived that the Lord had established him king over Israel, and that He had exalted his kingdom for His people Israel's sake (2 Samuel 5:11-12).

Hiram, the king of Tyre, saw the rising tide of destiny in David. David could no longer be penned in a box labeled "soldier"; he was now a head of state, and his nation would soon become the greatest nation in the near eastern world. Hiram, king of a small but wealthy nation, wanted to be in good relationship with the new king of the rapidly growing nation "next door."

That is why King Hiram began the same thing Abner did before his death, and the same thing the elders of Israel had done. He was "feathering his nest," getting himself in good relationship with the new "king of the mountain." While you need to let "outside" folks build business and social relationships with you, like Jesus, you can't fully commit yourself to people outside the Kingdom, because you know what is really in their hearts (see Jn. 2:23-24).

> *And David **perceived** that the Lord had established him king over Israel, and that He had exalted his kingdom for His people Israel's sake (2 Samuel 5:12).*

This verse describes the climax of David's life. We cannot overemphasize its importance. The Hebrew word for "perceive" is *yada.* This should be a familiar term by now. Again, *yada* means "to know, to understand, to comprehend." David realized that God had supernaturally brought him all the way from his father's fields, past Goliath, through the caves and battles, to the throne in Zion. What a day it must have been—the day David knew from deep inside that he was a significant part of God's eternal purpose. He perceived that God had made him king.

What did David do once he was in Zion? He immediately began to build a kingdom. That was good. But the Bible also says, "And David took him more concubines and wives out of Jerusalem, after he was come from Hebron: and there were yet sons and daughters born to David" (2 Sam. 5:13).

Can you see David's "Achilles' heel" or character weakness rise up again? He accumulated more wives, more women, more lovely faces, more warm bodies. David launches his new kingdom with a *mixture of good and bad.* "Wasn't it God's will for David to have sons and daughters and build the kingdom?" Absolutely. But David was nursing an unhealed wound. He was dealing with an unlearned lesson concerning intimacy. He was still longing for that marvelous woman named Merab, but she wasn't there.

And these be the names of those that were born unto him in Jerusalem; Shammuah, and Shobab, and Nathan, and Solomon, Ibhar also, and Elishua, and Nepheg, and Japhia, and Elishama, and Eliada, and Eliphalet (2 Samuel 5:14-16).

We don't hear anything from most of these sons, but we do hear about Solomon. These are the sons born to David's Jewish wives from Jerusalem. David also had a number of foreign wives (with idolatrous religious beliefs). One of them bore David a son named Absalom who was to create some very grave difficulties for him in the future.

When David perceived that the Lord had established him king over Israel, then he began to function. He needed to have a house. (I don't mean just a physical house, although you need one of those too. You need to have a family, and you need to have a home church.)

When God brought me to Columbus, Georgia, a number of years ago, He told me, "I want you to establish a local congregation that will be your family and your home.

You will be accountable to them, and they will be accountable to you as the father." I obeyed the Lord, and that local church family has been the stabilizing factor of this ministry as we reach around the world with ongoing ministry to 10 countries. Everything is based on the firm foundation of our home base, the local church.

"And David perceived that the Lord had established him king over Israel, and that He had exalted his kingdom for His people Israel's sake" (2 Sam. 5:12). David had an "inner awareness" that God had established, anointed, appointed, and sent him to Zion as king over Israel *for the people's sake*, not for his personal good. I like that. God "established" him. This is from the Hebrew word *kun*.

According to Zodhiates' *Hebrew/Greek Key Study Bible*, this word means "to bring something into incontrovertible existence."[1] The devil and his demon spirits have to deal with the reality of anything God establishes because its existence and authority are "incontrovertible." The same idea appears in the New Testament in the Book of First Corinthians:

> *But now hath God set the members* [of His body each and] *every one of them in the body, as it hath pleased Him. ... And God hath set some in the church, first apostles, secondarily prophets, thirdly teachers, after that miracles, then gifts of healings, helps, governments, diversities of tongues* (1 Corinthians 12:18,28).

---

1. Spiros Zodhiates, *The Hebrew-Greek Key Study Bible* (Chattanooga, TN: AMG Publishers, 1991), p. 1622.

The Greek word for "set," *tithemi*, is the equivalent of the Hebrew word *kun*. God "set" all these gift-anointings in the Body of Christ, just as He (not David) set, or established, David on the throne of Israel. The office of king in the Old Testament flows over into the apostolic office in the New Testament with some very interesting parallels. In this passage in Second Samuel, *kingdom* may be equated with the modern idea of a *ministry*. God established David's ministry.

Ministry is servanthood. In the Kingdom of God, the leader is the greatest servant of all (see Mk. 9:35). Most people draw the "hierarchy of leadership" like a pyramid, with the leader at the top. The Bible draws the hierarchy of leadership as an inverted pyramid. The Chief Cornerstone is Jesus Christ Himself at the base. Upon that He builds apostles, prophets, and evangelists, pastors, and teachers for the equipping of the saints. God declared:

> ...*I will pour out My spirit upon all flesh; and your sons and your daughters shall prophesy, your old men shall dream dreams, your young men shall see visions: and also upon the servants and upon the handmaids in those days will I pour out My spirit* (Joel 2:28-29).

God didn't say He would only call or speak through priests. He said He would speak through sons and daughters to declare His Word and give the message. That is powerful. (I teach a complete course on spiritual leadership that really goes into some depth on this subject.)

God established David "for Israel's sake" because He knew Israel needed David's ministry. When ministries are needed, God will raise them up if they are indeed willing to minister to the need. However, if they are going to take the talents or gifts and use them to line their own pockets, then God will deal with them. When a church congregation is worshiping God and a word of knowledge is given for someone who needs a healing, that means that God has prepared the gift of healing to flow in the Body.

God prepares ministry to meet need. There are more ministries being prepared today than at any other time in history, perhaps more than in all recorded history combined. People are beginning to sense that they are anointed and that they have been "set" in the Body of Christ for a definite purpose, a divine destiny. Remember, you don't "have" an anointing or gift, you *are* from before the foundation of the earth, a gift-anointing. I believe this is happening because we are on the verge of a great harvest! God knows He will need these ministries because He sees the harvest coming. My friend, we will be needed when it comes. The second reason God raised up David and established his ministry was for Israel's reward and blessing, to change them and make them better.

Can you see how different David is at this point compared to when he went into Adullam? Entering Adullam, he said, "I have to figure out what God is doing to me." Now he clearly perceived what God was doing. The Lord was establishing his kingdom as a permanent kingdom for Israel's sake. Despite David's increased powers of discernment and perception, there were still some deeper things that he couldn't see. I'm confident that David did not perceive that the lineage of the Messiah was in his loins or that the ultimate Kingdom God was establishing would be the Church of Jesus Christ, of which you and I are members today.

David's kingdom was established through the lowly tribe of Judah, for the true line of the tribe of Judah was within him. You never know the depth or quality of the oil in your cruse (or "earthen vessel") when God is involved. It is not your job to "understand" how deep the oil runs or flows; God knows. In terms of your faithfulness, your joy is to fulfill your divine destiny. Who knows whose life you'll touch who may become the messianic hope of his own generation and day.

A Boston Sunday school teacher named Edward Kimball went one day (April 21, 1855) to speak to a 19-year-old boy about his soul. He found the boy in the back of a store wrapping shoes in paper, preparing them to be sold. He simply told the boy of Christ's love for him and the love Christ wanted in return and asked him if he was ready to commit himself to Christ. To this simple appeal Dwight Lyman Moody surrendered his life. In later years Moody said this experience meant that "the old sun shone brighter than ever before, and I fell in love with the singing of the birds.... It seemed I was in love with all creation."[2]

That Sunday school teacher probably fulfilled his destiny that day! It didn't seem like much at the time, but he brought spiritual birth to a man who took cities for God

---

2. J.C. Pollock, *Moody* (New York, N.Y.: The Macmillan Co., 1963), p. 13-14.

with such power and annointing that thousands upon thousands fell on their faces surrendering to the God preached by Moody. Kimball will have his reward in all that Moody did.

Two things followed in quick succession once David knew what God was doing. First, David learned how to "build the church." And second, David learned how to defeat the enemy. We are to do the same today: Build the church and defeat the enemy.

The first thing to do when you obtain your ministry in Zion is to build up the local church. Now David tried to do the right thing the wrong way when he took more concubines and wives out of Jerusalem. Jerusalem was his destiny (that is your local church). He found desirable concubines and wives in his destiny to help him raise up a kingdom. This is obviously a very limited analogy at this point, yet it has some strengths. No minister alive can build a church *alone*. There must be "spiritual wives and concubines" who will "bear young and reproduce God's seed."

When I was 15 years old, like most boys, I was into athletics. But my first love was somewhere else. Every day after my high school classes were over and my athletic team practices were complete, I made a "bee line" to the front door of the church. I would ask my pastor, "What have you got for me to do today?" Many years later, when he had no teeth and was bent over and walking with a cane, this man of God told me, "Son, you pert' nigh killed me! Every day, I'd have to stop for a few minutes and think, *Now what can I do to keep that Cottle boy off of my back for the rest of the day?*" You see, even as a young boy in school, I caught a glimpse of the divine blueprint of my life and I felt a touch of the anointing. I wanted my destiny in God, so I became my pastor's "spiritual concubine," or one of his "spiritual wives" in the Kingdom (now don't run off and make this teaching analogy into some kind of off-beat doctrine!). Each time I went to him, this man of God would point me in a direction, give me a gentle shove with a word of encouragement, or just a pat on the head.

Each Friday, the preacher ran off 500 fliers on his old-fashioned mimeograph machine (an early version of the copy machine). The following morning, I was there by eight o'clock, and he put those fliers in my hand, telling me, "Now, son, I'm going to get in my Buick a little bit later, and I'm going to come along the route. Now I don't want to find two fliers at any one house."

Every Saturday, his son and I took those 500 fliers and loaded the whole community down with them. We used to drop them off in what used to be a restaurant and pharmacy that made milk shakes and malts. After we "fueled up" with a malt or shake, we'd start up again and distribute the rest of those fliers. This pattern went on for years. My pastor was using me to build the Kingdom. We are all to build up the local church.

David could not build God's family alone. He needed partners and helpers. We need sons and daughters in the Kingdom today, and you can't have them without spiritual partners to help birth them.

The second thing David learned after he learned to build a church was how to defeat the enemy. Second Samuel 5:17-25 outlines an interesting story about the Philistines' reaction to David's ascension to the throne of Israel.

"But when the Philistines heard that they had anointed David king over Israel, all the Philistines came up to seek David..." (2 Sam. 5:17). These Philistines weren't coming up to congratulate David; they were coming to kill him. Isn't this incredible? You would think that since David had come into power, the Philistines would be scared. They weren't.

We may not wrestle against Philistines in our day, but we do wrestle against principalities and powers. Listen, it doesn't matter how big or how powerful you get in church circles, or even how knowledgeable you become in biblical matters: the demon spirits, carnal nature, and old traditions in everyone's life die hard! They will camp on your doorstep even while you're praying in other tongues! They will challenge you right in the holy of holies of your life because they are not afraid. Their consciences are seared, and they are already doomed for hell. All they want to do is take you with them. No, we don't need to live in fear, but we shouldn't live in pride and presumption either!

David was seated on his throne of destiny and building his kingdom when his enemies came against him. Look closely at what he did then:

> ...*all the Philistines came up to seek David; and David heard of it, and went down to [masada] the hold* (2 Samuel 5:17).

Do you recall our discussion of *masada* versus *masuda*? When David went to Adullam, he made the hardest place of his life into a *masada*, a fortress, a test to make him better, rather than a *masuda*, which is a temptation to make him bitter. He took that *masada*, that inner fortress, with him wherever he went.

When the Philistines came to Jerusalem with their armies, David went to the physical *masada* or fortress at the heart of Jerusalem. This was the briefing room where he went to get a *rhema* or revelation from his general, the Holy Spirit of God. This is a magnificent story. David went down into the hold, and into the "briefing room" to get ahold of God. While his enemies, "The Philistines also came and spread themselves in the valley of Rephaim" (2 Sam. 5:18). The valley of *Rephaim* was literally the "valley of the giants," because the Hebrew word *rephaim* means "giant."

And David inquired of the Lord, saying, Shall I go up to the Philistines? wilt Thou deliver them into mine hand? And the Lord said unto David, Go up: for I will doubtless deliver the Philistines into thine hand (2 Samuel 5:19).

God said He would deliver David's enemies into his *yad* or "hand." This means He would deliver them "into David's *authority*"! He was saying, "David, they will be walking in the palm of your hand. I will deliver them into your authority."

And David came to Baal-perazim, and David smote them there, and said, The Lord hath broken forth upon mine enemies before me, as the breach of waters. Therefore he called the name of that place Baal-perazim. And there they left their images, and David and his men burned them (2 Samuel 5:20-21).

"And David came to Baal-perazim...." The word *perazim* means "the breaking of the wave on the shore." It is the tidal wave coming against the land. Baal was the god of the Philistines. When the Philistines camped around him, David went down into his *masada* to draw upon all his strength and past experiences with God. He received a *rhema* from God: "Go get them, David. I'll deliver them into your authority. Go for it, David!"

When David came out, the Bible says he came out like a tidal wave against the god of the Philistines! That is why he named the place *Baal-perazim*. "...And David smote them there, and said, The Lord hath broken forth upon mine enemies before me, as the breach of waters. Therefore he called the name of that place *Baal-perazim* [the breaking forth of the tidal wave upon my enemy]" (2 Sam. 5:20).

Now *that* is the way to fight spiritual warfare! When the enemy encamps round about you, when he taunts and tempts you, or tries to traumatize you, you need to get down into the hold. Now, if you have let past experiences and challenges turn into a *masuda*, then you don't have a hold or fortress. But if you can turn it into a *masada*, it will prove to be a mighty fortress to rebut every attack of the enemy!

Epilogue

Anointed to Reign, Required to Train

In his book, *Destined for the Throne*, Paul Billheimer wrote about the lives of people like you and me. He said that what really characterizes Christians is their destiny: *They are not destined for destruction; they are destined for a throne.* You and I are destined for a throne. We were born kings and queens. Even if your earthly mother thinks you were a "biological accident," your heavenly Father knows better.

You are no accident. Like David, you were, indeed, born a rising king or queen in the Kingdom of God! I love Peter's bold declaration to the Church:

But ye are a chosen generation, a royal priesthood, an holy nation, a peculiar people; that ye should shew forth the praises of Him who hath called you out of darkness into His marvellous light (1 Peter 2:9).

We are a chosen generation. God chose and secluded us for a special blessing because we are a royal priesthood.

I love to preach on the priesthood of the believer, but in spite of all those Sunday sermons, we almost always *forget* that we are a *royal* priesthood! That means that we're not just priests; we are *king-priests*. Peter's epistle was probably written in Greek, but his declaration appeared long before his day in the Hebrew and Aramaic passages of the Old Testament! It was embodied in the name and ministry of a mysterious king-priest of Abraham's day.

The Hebrew word for "king" is *melek*. The word for "righteous" is *zadok*. Abraham paid tithes and did reverence to the first king-priest recorded in the Bible, *Melchizedek*, the "King of Righteousness" who was literally the King of Salem (peace), and the priest (*kohen*) of the Most High. According to Peter, we are all *melchizedeks*, kings of righteousness through Christ Jesus.

We are a holy nation and *peculiar* people. That doesn't necessarily mean we're weird (although some of us are). The Greek word is *peripoieomai*. *Peri* means "all the way around," like *peri*meter. The other word, *poieses*, means "shaped." So peculiar people are "shaped all around," as His own special possession. God has fashioned us all the way around in every single detail to be *melchizedeks*, to be a holy nation of king-priests, a chosen generation. God left nothing to chance.

You may be thinking of your spouse or a friend with the unspoken question: *Well, why did the Lord make him like that then?* The answer is, God loves a challenge. He enjoys a great opportunity. If He made you, your spouse, or your "peculiar" friend perfect to start with, then He wouldn't have anything else to do. God loves a challenge.

God has not made any mistakes. No, He wasn't the victim of an accident when He created you. He says of you, just as He declared to the prophet Jeremiah long ago: "Before I formed thee in the belly I [already] *knew* thee" (Jer. 1:5a). The Hebrew word for "knew" is *yada*. It means "I recognized you; I designated you; I appointed you." You already had a divine appointment in the mind of God from before the foundations of the world! You are not an accident. You weren't created just to fill up the world. The world was created so that you would have a place to become your destiny. You are more important than the world.

The Lord also said, "...And before thou camest forth out of the womb I *sanctified* thee..." (Jer. 1:5). The Hebrew word for "sanctified" is *qadash*. It means, "I set you apart. I had a special reason and a purpose for you. I dedicated you. I chose and secluded you." Think about this: before God ever presented you to the world, He had nine months alone with you in your mother's womb as He fashioned and built you cell by cell, according to a divine blueprint He ordained before the foundations of the world. You may not like yourself, or at the very least, you would never call yourself "fabulous, fantastic, wonderful, and awesome." Yet you are!

Isn't it sad how we seem to get religious about everything? The act of "sanctifying" something isn't religious. When God chose and secluded you, he *sanctified*, or set you apart, for a purpose. The Hebrew word *kun* is translated *ordain* in the Bible. It simply means "I made you ready for your destiny in every single detail." Remember,

God knew your destiny before the foundation of the world. He formed you in your mother's body for that destiny. By the time you were fashioned and came forward at birth, you were absolutely and impeccably ready for that destiny! You had all the ingredients inside you that were necessary to be what God called you to be.

David was 17 years old when he was anointed by Samuel (some scholars say that he might have been 14). Assuming he was 17 years old the day he was anointed, David's life moved in approximate seven-year stages from that point on. After he returned to his father's sheep in the wilderness, he wrote several psalms describing what God had done within him. He was overwhelmed with a new vision of God's love and destiny for him:

> *When I consider Thy heavens, the work of Thy fingers, the moon and the stars, which Thou hast ordained; what is man, that Thou art mindful of him? and the son of man, that Thou visitest him? For Thou hast made him a little lower than the angels, and hast crowned him with glory and honour. Thou madest him to have dominion over the works of Thy hands; Thou hast put all things under his feet* (Psalm 8:3-6).

David was "waxing eloquent" because he had recognized what God could do with any individual who was completely committed to Him.

Your destiny sets you apart. Before God ever formed you in the womb, indeed before He ever put a gleam in your daddy's eye and a willingness in your mama's heart, He already knew you. He had already *peri-poiesied* you, or fashioned you all the way around in every single detail. He already had you in His mind. Before you came out of the womb (many scholars think that this means *in utero*, or in the uterus), something magnificent happened. God was there molding you with His own skilled hands, while you were going through the process of mitosis (cell division), and in each embryonic and fetal stage. It is a fact that God has sanctified and ordained the birth of every single human being.

When you emerged from the womb and entered the world, you arrived according to God's intricate blueprint, a detailed diagram created by and known to God before the foundation of the world—a design for destiny. What an exciting thought. Can we prove it from the Bible? I think we can.

God told Jeremiah, "Before I *formed* thee..." (Jer. 1:5). The Hebrew word for "formed" is *yatsar*. This word has a lot of meanings, but in this passage it literally means "to shape." Another key Hebrew word about your destiny is *raqam*, which means "to embroider." In Psalm 139, David wrote:

> *My substance was not hid from Thee, when I was made in secret, and curiously **wrought** in the lowest parts of the earth. Thine eyes did see my substance, yet being unperfect; and in Thy book all my members were written, which in continuance were fashioned, when as yet there was none of them* (Psalm 139:15-16).

I believe David wrote this psalm shortly after Samuel anointed him king. David didn't reign immediately after his anointing *because he had to train first*. It was in the wilderness that he began to have great revelations, and it was there that he wrote Psalm 139. When he wrote, "I was made in secret, and curiously *wrought*..." he was saying, "I was curiously *raquam* (or embroidered)." When he said, "Thine eyes did see my *substance*, yet being unperfect," he used the Hebrew word *golem*, which means "unwrapped or unformed substance," as "an embryo."

I taught these things in a Bible study not long ago, and several medical doctors and an embryologist in my audience came up to me afterward and said, "We never saw this." I answered, "Yes, and the Church never saw it either." Hippocrates, who is considered the father of modern medicine, came along in 400 B.C. David wrote his psalm on the "embroidery of God on the unwrapped form of man" in 1200 B.C., 800 years before the advent of "modern" medicine! Ironically, David's revelation in Psalm 139 still outstrips our current understanding of what really goes on in the birth process!

For Thou hast possessed my reins: Thou hast covered me in my mother's womb. I will praise Thee; for I am fearfully and wonderfully made: marvellous are Thy works; and that my soul knoweth right well (Psalm 139:13-14).

David declared, "You *possessed* my reins and covered me in my mother's womb." David knew something that we're just now discovering in modern medicine according to the doctors who came up to talk with me. The Hebrew word for "possess" is *qanah*. It means "to create, to own, to literally build or erect a thing piece by piece."

When David said, "Oh, God, You possessed my *reins*," he used the Hebrew word *kilyah*, which means "my inner being." David received a great revelation here. He was saying, "You covered me." That means "You hedged me about and shut me up in my mother's womb while you built me line upon line, part by part."

He almost seems to stop and throw up his hands as he suddenly says, "I will praise You!" We know this because the word translated as "praise" in this passage is *yadah* (from *yad*), which means "to praise with hands extended." When you praise the Lord with your hands lifted with the palms outward, you are in a posture of surrender, giving God the authority (*yad*) over your life.

Now the Hebrew language has two words for hand, the first being *yad*. The second word *kaph* describes worship to God with the palms directed upward toward Heaven. This puts you in the posture to receive what God has for you. It refers to the grasping element of the hand.

David was saying, "I will praise You with my hands extended—*yadah*—in total submission to You. You are greater than I am." Now watch what David says about himself, and don't ever put yourself down again! According to the King James Version, David declared, "I am fearfully and wonderfully made."

The Hebrew word wrongly translated "fearfully" is *yare'*. The blunt truth is that it means "awesome"! David was saying, "I am awesome, God!" When you say, "I am awesome," it means "to be reverenced." We should reverence ourselves because God "*qanah'*ed," or erected, us cell by cell by cell! We're no accident. God did it from the very beginning. The very moment the sperm and the egg met, God took over and "erected" us according to His own pre-determined blueprint.

Then David says, "I am awesome and *wonderfully* made!" or "I am *pala'*!" The Hebrew word means, "I am made with a difference, I am a miracle set apart as a marvelous show!" David clearly knew he was not "naturally evolved." You can't believe this passage and be an evolutionist! Like David, you can declare, "I am not naturally evolved. I am specially, miraculously generated!" Now that is powerful.

David went on to say, "*Marvelous* are Thy works." What are these "works" he was talking about? Every commentator I have read says, "David looked at the heavens and said, 'Marvelous are Thy works.' " No, I have to disagree. David had just completed a lengthy commentary of praise to God on the wonders of his own being. He was simply summing it all up when he said, "*Marvelous* are Thy works, O God!"

Now it's your turn. You should step in front of a mirror, lift your hands to your Maker, and say, "Oh God, You have done a marvelous thing here! A marvelous thing!"

The Hebrew word for "marvelous" is *pala*. It means "unique, one-of-a-kind, hand-made, distinguished from all other models." Isn't that fantastic? "There is only one of you!"

David gave us a clue about the timing of this psalm when he said, "...And that my soul [my *nephesh*, my inner man] *knoweth right well*" (Ps. 139:14). He was saying, "I have come to recognize this because I have felt the anointing. I caught a glimpse of the divine destiny within me. I know who I am. I know why I'm here. I know what my purpose is. I will not follow these sheep around forever. God has a destiny for me."

My substance was not hid from Thee, when I was made in secret, and curiously wrought in the lowest parts of the earth. Thine eyes did see my substance, yet being un-perfect; and in Thy book all my members were written, which in continuance were fashioned... (Psalm 139:15-16).

Where did this miracle take place? The King James Version gives us a really poor translation when it says, "...in the lowest parts of the earth." The Hebrew word is *tachtiy*. It literally means "in the earliest beginnings of my being, in the depths of my mother's womb, when the sperm and the egg first came together." At this earliest moment God already had your blueprint formed, fashioned, and ready. Everything that happened in those nine months of God's preparation were orchestrated according to a divine blueprint of God's making! David puts it this way: "...and in Thy *book* [*kaphar*, cipher or "blueprint"], all my members were written." God had your blueprint long before the worlds were made, and it included everything that occurred in your development before the doctor ever slapped you on your rump and handed you to your mother!

This is the background and the basis for our study of David, and our own training to fulfill our twofold divine destiny of "being" and of "doing."

For a long time, I believed my divine destiny was out-lined in the Book of Romans:

And we know that all things work together for good to them that love God, to them who are the called according to His purpose. For whom He did foreknow, He also did predestinate to be conformed to the image of His Son, that He might be the firstborn among many brethren (Romans 8:28-29).

I have always thought, *I am predestined to be like Jesus. My blueprint is to be like Jesus*; and that's right. But it includes more than that! Once again, we need to return to the verse we quoted earlier, Jeremiah 1:5: "Before I formed thee in [thy mother's womb] I knew thee; and before thou camest forth out of [your mother's] womb I sanctified thee, and I ordained thee...[what?]...a *prophet* unto the nations."

Jeremiah was the fifth great prophet in the history of Israel. The four who went before him were prophets to Israel, or to Israel and Judah only. They were not "international" prophets. Why was Jeremiah different? Why was he called as an international prophet? Nebuchadnezzar came along and destroyed Jerusalem and the nation of Israel. Ezekiel was taken to Babylon, and Jeremiah was left. Jeremiah then became the prophet to all the nations out there in the Dispersion.

God knew that before He ever formed Jeremiah in the womb of his mother, Nebuchadnezzar would disperse the Jews among the nations. He knew that Jeremiah was going to be a special, one-of-a-kind prophet.

God knows all about you, too. He knows the circumstances that have come into your life. Yet you have this confidence: Nothing can ever influence you that doesn't have a nail-scarred handprint on it! God is in charge of your life. There is a divine design inside of you that will become your ultimate destiny as it is worked out in your world.

Since we are human, the first thing we did when we came into the world, was to "mess up the blueprint" in a big way. When we were born in His image, God said "Go and reproduce My image in the earth," and like little kindergarten children with tiny hands trying to manhandle those monster pencils designed for 300-pound football players, we just couldn't seem to "stay inside the lines." (Do you remember those pencils? They should be outlawed as a form of "cruel and inhumane punishment"!)

I remember the day I got my pencil and started trying to do my assignment to trace a human face on a thin sheet of paper laid over a pattern underneath. I couldn't do anything *but* miss the mark. I couldn't stay within the lines to save myself, and the more I missed it, the madder I got. Before long, I just scribbled all over it, and then I wet the paper with water and smeared it. When the teacher came along, I handed it to her in frustration and anger. Now, that's a picture of "original sin," isn't it?

When God said, "Go and trace Me," all any of us could do was "miss the mark." God's solution to our problem was to send Jesus. You and I messed up the blueprint of the likeness of God. Now the image of our Maker was still there. We didn't lose His image; we lost His likeness.

So God sent Jesus into the world, and Jesus traced the Father without missing the mark even once. "For we have not an high priest which cannot be touched with the feeling of our infirmities; but was in all points tempted like as we are, yet without sin" (Heb. 4:15).

He was tested, tried, and tempted in every manner like you and me. But Scripture says He was "without sin." The word for "sin" is *hamartia*, which means to "miss the mark." Jesus never "colored outside the lines." He perfectly outlined and described the Father before our eyes, and then He climbed on a tree and cried out, "tetelestai." That means, "It is finished." What was finished? The blueprint was restored! Jesus had perfectly etched the Father in the human race and restored the blueprint of His likeness in the family of man.

Now, the perfect man and woman that God had initially created was capable of being fulfilled. When Jesus ascended to Heaven, the Holy Spirit was waiting there like the "anchor runner" in a relay race. Jesus handed the restored image of God to the Holy Spirit, and the Spirit went on a "search and rescue" mission to the highways and byways of our world. He found you and me in our own personal pigsties—we were all "prodigal sons" who had ruined our lives.

In this process we call "conversion," the Holy Spirit took what God created, what you and I ruined, and what Jesus redeemed—the likeness of God, that divine destiny and divine design—and He planted it like a seed in your spirit man. Today, therefore, as a Christian, you have the capability of being everything God intended you to be from before the foundations of the world!

David was destined to be king of Israel. What is your destiny? David was anointed to reign, but he didn't reign until he had trained for his purpose. You are a gift anointing in the earth. Everything God wants of you, He has already put inside you. However, just as He said to David thousands of years ago, He is saying to you today, "Come on—you must train to reign. You have to get ready to occupy the throne of ministry and destiny to which I have called you."

David's life and training reveal three "classrooms" or training phases that we all must go through. Each "classroom" takes us through three lessons according to the precise pattern God gave us in David. When we pass through these three classrooms, we will go on to Zion, our destiny. That life-changing process is the heart and essence of this book, and it could very well become a turning point in your life and ministry.

Other

Destiny Image titles
you will enjoy reading